THE INCOMPARABLE,
ICONIC, AND IRREVERENT:

IRIS APFEL

29 AUGUST 1921 – 1 MARCH 2024

'It has been an honour to
know and to learn from Iris.'
RUVÉN AFANADOR

'One of the industry's
oldest tastemakers.'
VOGUE

'The inimitable style icon.'
HARPER'S BAZAAR

'The O.G. geriatric
fashion inspiration.'
NEW YORK TIMES

'A force of nature.'
TOMMY HILFIGER

With you, our life is just a sea of bliss, A treasure!

IRIS APFEL

COLOURFUL

WHAT IS THE COLOUR OF HAPPINESS?

EBURY
PRESS

← **PAGE 1**

My friend Ruvén Afanador took this portrait for my 100th birthday in 2021. I'm wearing Giambattista Valli. I threw a party, of course.

↓ **THIS PAGE**

Design feeds my soul. I had the pleasure of designing rugs with Ruggable, which we first launched in 2022, and Ruvén shot this marvellous set-up. Creative work gives me life.

Contents

∞ **Introduction** — 009
Put on your glasses

1
Everything has an influence on everything else — 016
On creativity

2
I like happy colours — 082
On the power of colour

3
Never stop being bold and having fun — 130
On playfulness

4
Get comfortable outside your comfort zone — 184
On courage

5

You only have one trip. Enjoy it   212
On longevity

6

There's all kinds of beauty   244
On appreciation

7

What is the colour of happiness?   266
I have a few thoughts

Index   278

Picture credits   282

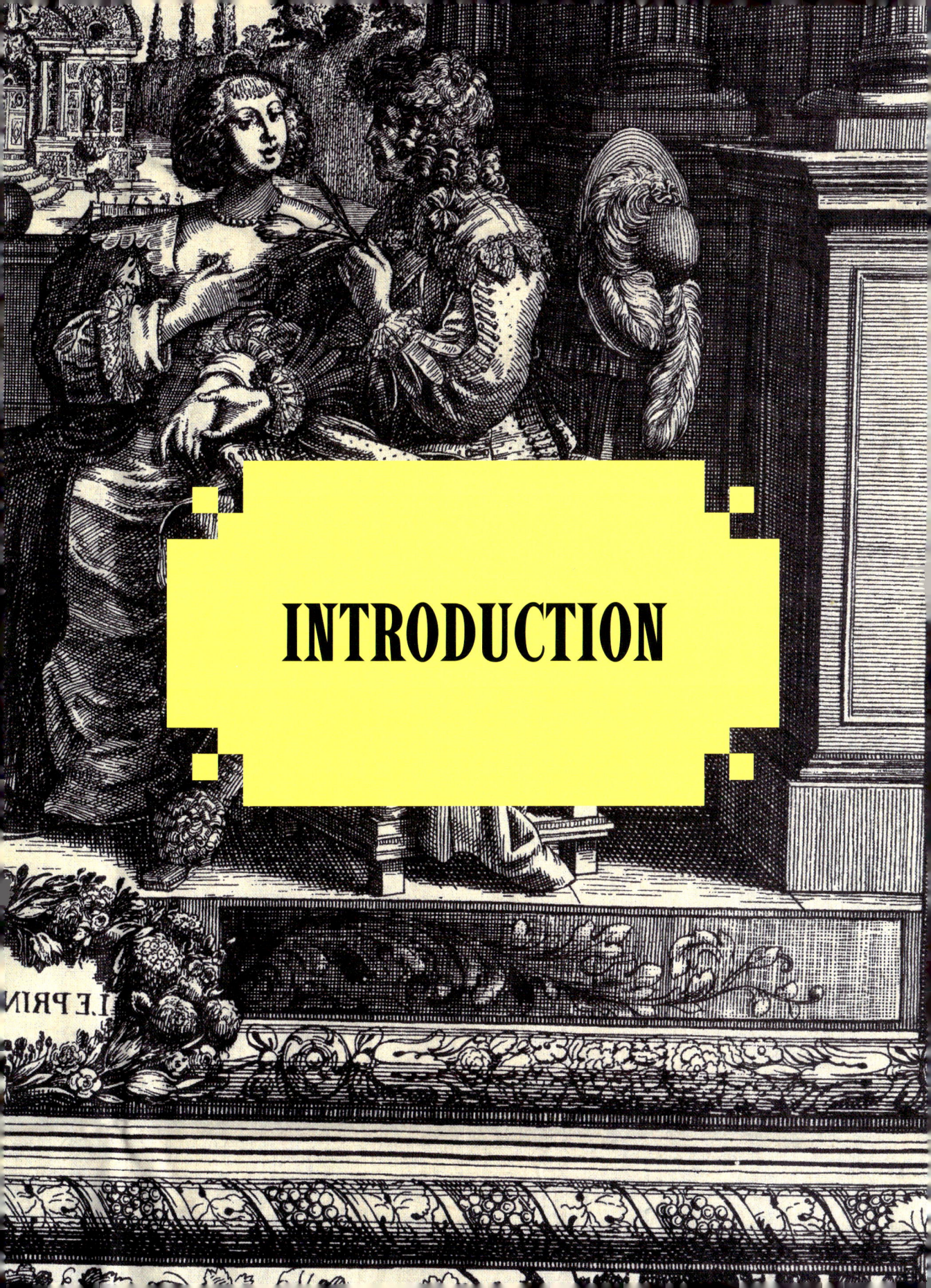

INTRODUCTION

Put on your glasses ⚭

FOR *Harper's Bazaar Arabia*
RICHARD PHIBBS
2021

This is not a book of secrets – I have no secrets. Sorry to disappoint if that's what you're looking for. I have some good stories though. And a few ideas.

This book is about living. Creating. Colouring life. The colours of life.

I enjoy life. I think living is wonderful, and I'm so thankful for the life I have lived. If I could remain one age forever, I wouldn't. I don't believe in that. I enjoy being alive. I enjoy people. I enjoy experience. I enjoy work. There is very little I don't enjoy. Perhaps that's the secret?

Enjoy as much as you can.

Much love,
Iris

→ FROM MY COLLECTION

Every piece has a story. Every one brightens my life.

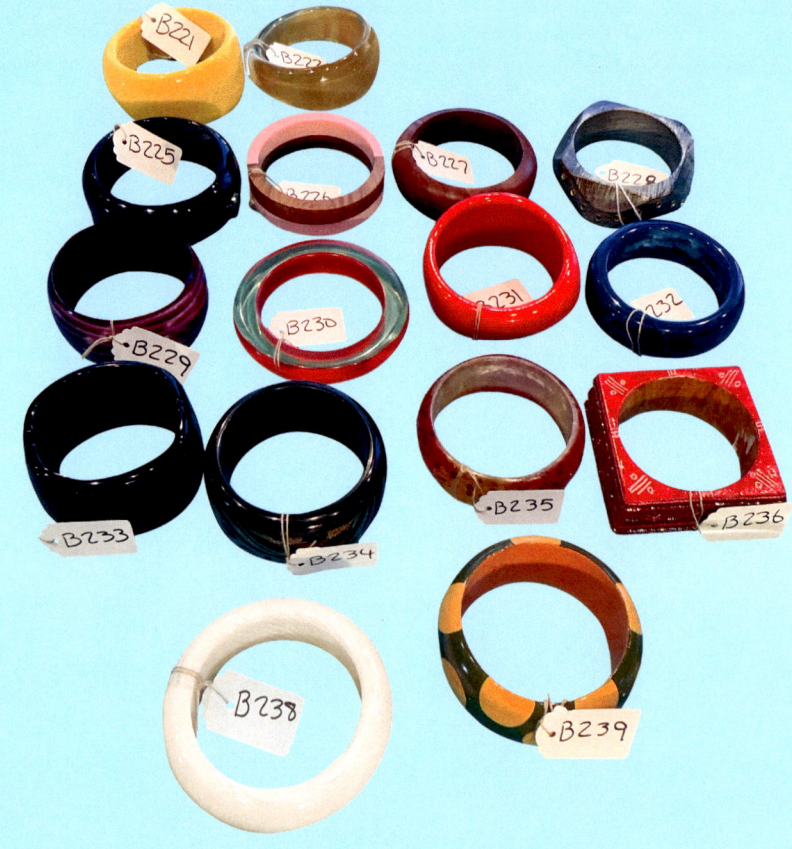

Live in technicolour.

Why?

Because colour matters. It stimulates something inside us. It has a certain effect on how we think, feel, see the world. It affects our personalities. The colours that resonate with us are a visual representation of our personalities.

Me, I'm primarily cheerful Chinese red and turquoise blue – but not only and not always. What about you?

Life is a rainbow.

We need colour in our lives because life can be very drab – on the worst days, an absolute wasteland. Colour adds … pep. Colour adds dignity.

Colour is an integral part of all the good things that you're living. And it makes the not-so-good-things more palatable too. I think we need it more than ever.

I think colour is one of the greatest things that we have to draw on, to live with, to be inspired by. I can't live without it. It is a precious gift to be used wisely, because it has the power to influence your life.

Life is any and every colour you choose. Life is almost anything you want to make it, please believe that for yourself.

As well as colour, I have also always been obsessed with texture and pattern. I think these represent the different facets of your life. Experiences are the textures and patterns in your life.

I don't want you to dress like me, and I don't want you to think like me – that's not the idea of this book. I want you to think for yourself, to find the colours, confidence and creative inspiration that reflects you. Explore your imagination. Believe in your gut feeling. I go by it, and I swear by it. Wear what you love. Live how you choose. Go confidently and with authenticity!

My life has been filled with love, wonder and a very deep, incurable curiosity. This book is my treasure trove of inspiration, influences and ideas. My source.

→ ME, PALM BEACH, 1948

Find your source.

Be your own style icon.

What makes you happy?

1
EVERYTHING HAS AN INFLUENCE

On creativity

Simply said, imitation is a sincere form of flattery.

Part of staying young is to keep learning, so I consider myself a life-long student. Nothing and no one exists in a creative vacuum, at least not in my life.

Everything (and everyone) is inspiration. Even bad experience is good inspiration.

FOR ZENNI OPTICAL
RUVÉN AFANADOR
2021

As I said earlier, experience is the texture and pattern that makes a life interesting. You don't want a smooth blank canvas, do you?

As Auntie Mame always said, *'Don't procrastinate. Nothing takes the place of experience.'*

Life is a banquet.

↙ ALWAYS EXPLORING

Four decades of travelling with friends in America, Europe and North Africa, seeking souks, bazaars, flea markets ... and a good breakfast spot.

EVERYTHING HAS AN INFLUENCE

The patterns in my life represent different adventures I've had – from the souks and bazaars of North Africa, to European flea markets, to some of America's most stylish homes. Style can be a physical manifestation of your spirit, and pattern seems to express mine. I have always worn and surrounded myself with pattern. It's like the layers of a personality. And that can be the personality of a place as much as a person.

Putting together the elements of an interior or an ensemble are one and the same. You draw on your experience, including your thoughts and feelings, and your likes and dislikes. It's the same sensibility, the same aesthetic.

And I think a house should reflect the people who live there every bit as much as clothing does.

← MY FAVOURITE RED NEVER FAILS
Attending an awards party in New York, 2016.

I go from my antique Chinese robes, to Ralph Rucci evening jackets, to floral pieces hand-painted by Gianni Versace himself. I like the French provincial style, my dear friend Duro Olowu's designs, which draw on his Nigerian heritage, and my Indian-inspired paisley-motif jacket, which I've made in countless different colourways. I have a nineteenth-century evening cape in paisley, too – it's beautiful. I love all the vibrant patterns of silks from the Arabian Peninsula, Native American craftsmanship and traditional North African rug motifs … and Venetian painted furniture. Oh my God, it drives me nuts.

I'm experimental. I like to mix up everything … offbeat things from different places, different times.

I've had to cut down in a big way, because I've run out of wall space, but I'm still surrounded with pattern in paintings and posters of past exhibitions, and treasures from my travels like weavings, pitchers, bowls, vases, you name it. My love binds it all together.

→ MAKE LIFE A SPECTACLE

Surround yourself with what you love. Ruvén Afanador, 2021.

My travel has inspired me always. For as long as I can remember, I was absorbing every day, seeing and learning, in every place. Everything is influence. That's life. Living is what you absorb and see every day. I am a sponge;

I learn from osmosis. Soaking up and absorbing ideas all the time, things I don't realise I am taking in.

I store it all away until the moment I need it, and then it pops out.

As an interior decorator, I travelled all around the world, seeking out one-of-a-kind pieces, and later with my husband Carl ♡, researching and sourcing fabrics for our manufacturing company Old World Weavers. Setting foot on European soil in the early 1950s changed my life forever. Oh, the architecture of London and Paris – I adored it. Italy, Greece. Then we went further afield to Lebanon, Turkey, Morocco, Pakistan, you name it. But we didn't have the opportunity to go to India.

↑   CARL♡ – A FIRST TRIP TOGETHER
Arriving off the RMS Mauretania, West Indies, 1959.

→   YUM YUM

← THE OLD WORLD WEAVERS SHOWROOM

I wish I'd gone there. I love Indian craftmanship, the colours and patterns. It influenced my designs, but I had to find that inspiration through books and reading and museums – we didn't have the chance to go. That's a pattern missing in my life. But it didn't stop me going there many, many times in my imagination.

Style and design are forever connected.

If you ask me what makes a good pattern, I would say balance. Design, for me, starts with an idea, that I play with – improvise with. I never know what's going to happen until it feels right and I know we've arrived at something good. That's what makes design exciting.

The inspiration I drew on most when Carl ♡ and I had Old World Weavers came from the late-seventeenth, eighteenth, nineteenth and early-twentieth centuries. We found interesting old designs and replicated them. There was no rulebook for replicating the patterns and colours, so that was the fun of it – we had to connect the dots, then pick the colours. I'm very visceral about what I do; there are still no rules. Not everyone can work like that, but it suits me.

OLD WORLD WEAVERS, INC

EVERYTHING HAS AN INFLUENCE 33

Art has always been a big influence in my life. I studied history of art, and was exposed to many ideas early on – not just art, but architecture and all different aspects of culture – from ballet (Mother was a balletomane and dragged me to performances at a very tender age) to classical music. I think that must have influenced my obsession with movement, colour and pattern.

I think the beginning of my fascination with different cultural and historic influences began long before art school.

My father did me a big favour when I was growing up, by insisting that if I really wanted to succeed in the world, I had better meet and understand what every kind of person was about.

→ MY DARLING PARENTS THROUGH THE DECADES
We became great friends and travelling companions.

EVERYTHING HAS AN INFLUENCE 35

↓   MA AND PA, 1940

I was no better than anyone else. My father resisted my mother's plans to send me to an elegant school with a greater chance of admission to an Ivy League college, and I shall never stop thanking him for that lesson. It made good sense then, and the importance of openness and curiosity shaped my life.

It would be wrong to say that one era in art and design was entirely good, or to write off another era entirely. I love everything with a sense of baroque.

Personally, I don't like Art Nouveau, but I can appreciate that some wonderful things came out of it. I'm always surprised to see animal prints coming back. Everything has its good and bad sides. There are lots of shades of grey in the world – you can't think in black and white.

I love some very simple styles, but I also love what's big and bold. One informs the other. I like to go between them, mixing things up.

I'd love to have seen the sixth century, when Istanbul was Constantinople – the heart of the Byzantine Empire.

The art and the patterns from that time were complete knockouts.

I have a lot in common with some artists in my approach to colour. When Tate Modern had an exhibition on Henri Matisse and his cutouts, we explored parallels with the way I dress. The curators thought I had a similar approach to combining vivid colours, and I realised they were right.

Matisse must have been influencing me all this time without my knowing it. One of the cutouts I love, *The Snail*, is an example of the tonality I love. The brightly coloured squares are sort of smoked down, a bit subdued, and they blend beautifully.

Fashion editors talk about colour blocking today, but Matisse was doing it all along. He also loved jazz, like me, and when I think of him cutting and improvising with magnificent, intense colours, it all makes a lot of sense to me.

← MY 100TH BIRTHDAY PARTY, 2021
I wore canary yellow, of course, from my H&M collection. It was pure joy.

Our own textile designs at Old World Weavers were classic, but over the top. We worked with the White House for so many years to restore and recreate historic fabrics that I got the nickname '*First Lady of Fabric*', or '*Our Lady of the Cloth*'. Which is quite funny, because I ended up with quite a collection of vintage and antique vestments in my closet. They had fabulous colours and details.

Back in the early fifties, when a flea market was really a flea market, I found a well-preserved nineteenth-century ruby-red silk Lyonnaise velvet priest's tunic at one of my favourite textile stalls in the Marché aux Puces in Paris. As antique fabrics went, this was one to make you swoon. It had a large insert of a beautiful silk broché with marvellous braiding, and was completely eye-popping. It had never been worn.

Carl ♡ insisted I didn't need any old clothes. He thought it would look like we couldn't afford a real dress. But I had to have it. I knew it would make the most wonderful cocktail attire. Luckily, Eugenia Sheppard, the fashion critic, came by at the perfect moment. She gasped and made a fuss of it and Carl ♡ calmed down. I duplicated the fabric for our Old World Weavers line and got some matching trousers and slippers too. The whole outfit came in handy when attending various black-tie dos at the White House. I've never worn anything so much.

Nature is the best designer in the world.

FOR *Harper's Bazaar Arabia*
RICHARD PHIBBS
2021

I love the frivolity of feathers.

↑   GIRAFFE PRINT COAT, 1965

I bought this coat in Paris. I'm wearing it on a boat somewhere on the Arabian Sea.

EVERYTHING HAS AN INFLUENCE

← CAPRI, ITALY

A French friend came from Paris with great news that French are drinking red wine with white fish, 1950s.

↓ INSPIRED BY NATURE TO MAKE A STATEMENT

EVERYTHING HAS AN INFLUENCE

→ MOTHER NATURE KNOWS BEST

I agree with her, I don't like matchy-matchy *'sameness'* either.

↓ FISHING...

...for inspiration, Miami Beach, 1938.

I had to learn to love unconventional pairings, though. When I was about four years old, I caused a bit of an incident when we were on vacation at some resort. I shrieked the place down because my mother put a ribbon in my hair that didn't match my outfit. I howled and howled, but of course my mother knew best.

Look up and down at the flowers, plants, birds and animals, and in the ocean for the answers. It's all there waiting.

EVERYTHING HAS AN INFLUENCE

Nature knows everything.

It provides us with so much. It's a gift.

Layering patterns and colours makes me feel alive.

Alive to the world.
Part of the world.
It's natural.

Don't overthink it.

Every work is
not a creation. Some
things just happen.

In 2023, I created a collection of rugs with a homeware brand called Ruggable and I poured all of my life's inspiration into the designs. It was such fun. I just love dressing a space and considering how many ways I can bring joy and fun into a room. Design work feeds my soul. Knowing I might make a positive change in someone's home is a great pleasure for me.

The world is so full. There are so many things to be inspired by. What inspires you?

← ON SAFARI

I have a memory of my mother having a zebra skin – she was crazy for it. I thought it would be fun to create a rug inspired by this memory. No zebras were harmed in the making of this one.

→ THE CZARDAS RUG

This pattern was named after a Hungarian folk dance and is inspired by eighteenth-century Hungarian textile patterns. It has an energy to it, like the dance.

↑ FLUTTERBY

I think butterflies denote happiness, they are a flutter of colourful beauty: joyful, fun.

FUN, FUN, FUN.
WE HAVE TO
HAVE FUN.

MORE IS MORE
AND LESS IS
A BORE.

Know yourself and stay true to that. Mrs Loehmann, the godmother of discount shopping, was the first person who told me I had something special. She was a remarkable teacher. I discovered her store, Loehmann's, in Brooklyn, one rainy day in my late twenties, just after I was married. I'd heard about it, but when I saw the exalted *'back room'*, I was dizzy with excitement. It was full of truly great clothing designers at incredibly low prices, and it was like I'd died and gone to heaven.

Mrs Loehmann was a visionary. This was back in the days of the deep depression when everybody else was going out of business. She kept Seventh Avenue alive. She bought all these fantastic clothes and then sold them at a very small profit, establishing this incredible fashion business. She had lived in different places and was like a sponge, too, soaking up all the time, feeding her creativity. Every day she'd go to the market to see what she could find – all kinds of marvellous clothes that I never thought the likes of me would ever wear. But I was suddenly able to buy them. It was a revelation.

She was an absolute trip, Mrs Loehmann. She was a small woman who wore her hair in a topknot, had round spots of rouge on her cheeks, and always wore a high-necked, buttoned blouse, a long skirt with a drawstring belt and high button shoes. She looked like something out of a Toulouse-Lautrec painting. She would sit on a high stool as if she was umpiring a tennis match and watch everybody in the shop. I'd sashay about the shop and she would fixate on me.

One day she said,

'Young lady, I've been watching you. You're not pretty and you'll never be pretty. Don't let anybody ever con you into that. But it doesn't matter. You have something much better. You have style.'

→ HUNTING FOR TREASURES IN LOEHMANN'S

↓ OLD WORLD WEAVERS DAYS
I have found the ideal curtain tie-backs and I am delighted. Somewhere in France, 1950.

She was the first person who *saw* me.

Besides that, she taught me so much. What good fabric was. A lot about style and manufacture, and how things should be made. Many of the clothes she held were as beautiful inside as outside. She knew her stuff. I was always short of time in those days, and she had a policy of no returns, but the textiles were drop-dead, so I always figured if something didn't fit it could have another life as a throw pillow.

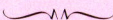

EVERYTHING HAS AN INFLUENCE

58 IRIS APFEL COLOURFUL

←   MILLICENT ROGERS

Photographed in 1947 after being voted one of the ten best dressers of the year by the New York Dress Institute.

↓   BE BOLD, BE BRAVE

I got my love of big, bold jewellery from Millicent.

I have to mention Millicent Rogers. She was a very, very wealthy oil heiress, a socialite, jewellery designer and art collector, and she dressed with perfection. A very interesting person. She was so original and unusual and never looked like anyone else. I lusted after her wardrobe. She was inspired by places and all kinds of art, and it influenced her style in so many interesting ways. Her taste went all over the map: from Austrian folk style, to Navajo dress, to Balenciaga. She had courage in her convictions. She collected Native American jewellery, which was very unusual back then.

Her collection is now at her museum in Taos, New Mexico. Carl ♡ and I used to go to that part of the world every summer, and we always made a pilgrimage to the museum to see that jewellery.

← **MAMA WAS PEPPY**
Sharing a joke with my Uncle Foxy.

My mother was a great influence on me. Her loves were completely different to mine. But she had great taste. She was very chic and dressed beautifully. Everything was always just so. She could do tricks with a scarf I've never seen anybody else do. I've always been an accessories freak; I caught that from my mother.

She knew what she wanted and she knew who she was. It really made an impression on me.

It's the most important thing about having a style: you have to know who you are. You've got to be very strict with your own foundation.

Mama also had a great sense of humour. She was peppy. She told the best off-colour jokes. She liked to work, and that's where I get my love of work from.

She praised my taste. Even though our tastes were different, she laid the groundwork. She encouraged me. It's important.

She was really quite exceptional for her time – she went to college and, for a time, to law school, and she was in real-estate before I was born.

EVERYTHING HAS AN INFLUENCE

I think I was 11 when she went back to work, opening a boutique in Long Island City, in Queens, during the Great Depression. She sold both expensive and inexpensive clothing and accessories, including lots of wonderful costume jewellery, and she did very well despite the times. I worked in her store, helping others become more colourful.

One Easter, when she was working – and in those days there was an Easter parade down Fifth Avenue – I had nothing to wear, so my mother said, *'I'll give you $25 and you can go shopping. You go on your own to see what you come back with.'*

↓ A RARE WARDROBE SHARE
Mama borrowed that dress from me and never returned it.

$25 wasn't bad for those days. The dinosaurs were roaming the Earth, and you could buy a lot more for your money. We discussed strategy. I went to Manhattan from Astoria on the subway, with the money in my hot little hand, and I bought a dress, shoes, a smashing straw hat and a pair of white gloves. I had a nice little lunch and took the subway home, well under budget. I fell madly in love with the dress right away, on the very first rack – it was a silk-tie print shirtmaker dress with glorious buttons and these big poet sleeves – but I said to myself, *'Oh, no, Mama says you have to comparison shop; you can't just buy the first thing you see.'* I had to balance it all.

My mother had felt badly that she had to work and couldn't accompany me, but it turned out for the best. It was quite an adventure! To have that opportunity, that little bit of freedom to try … When I got home, my mother praised my style sense, and my father praised my financial abilities. My grandpa, who was a master tailor, pronounced the buttonholes a disaster. But as long as he was in America and as long as I knew him, he never found a buttonhole he liked. Anyway, that was the first time I put an outfit together. My first foray into haute couture and high finance! And the beginning of my becoming a skillful shopper.

My mother, father, grandpa – they had strong opinions. I absorbed their ways.

My mother had a great eye for shopping on a shoestring. Everything she bought was discount because nobody had any money in those days. She was always collecting antique vases. My father was a senior-grade market freak and ardent traveller. He knew the price of cheese in every European capital city. He bought a lot of things from Germany – he used to have an office there. His family business was glass and mirrors. He did exquisite mirror work, and he had marvellous clients. He worked for a lot of top interior designers and that put the bug of interior design in my head. He also imported children's stuffed animals and musical instruments from Germany in the 1920s for Barhep Imports and Exports Corp – beautiful, incredible dolls and toys. My parents collected. That's where I got it from.

↓ SOME OF MAMA'S ADORED PORCELAIN

Dearest Honey,

Ever roaming, roaming on. On the trains and off again. In one city and out again. Like a perpetual pendulum from one to the other but today dear is the 13th — and heavily will the other days pass till the 22nd and then one long voyage + home sweet home. Love to all

Sam

← LETTER FROM PA TO MA

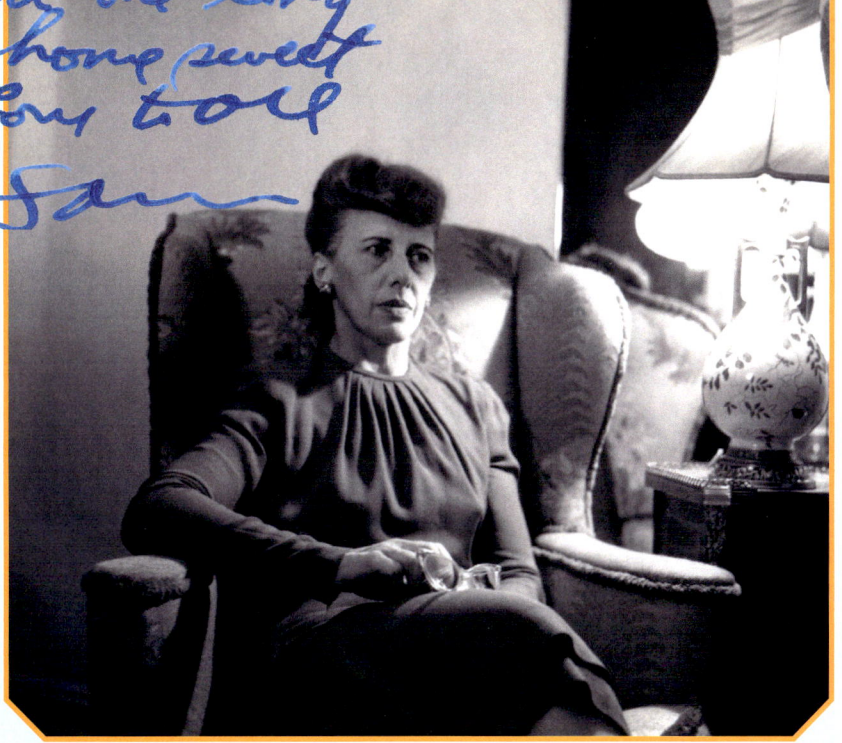

EVERYTHING HAS AN INFLUENCE

I bargain hunt, and I still love it. It was necessity and then, as life moved forward, it became amusing. I just love the thrill of the hunt.

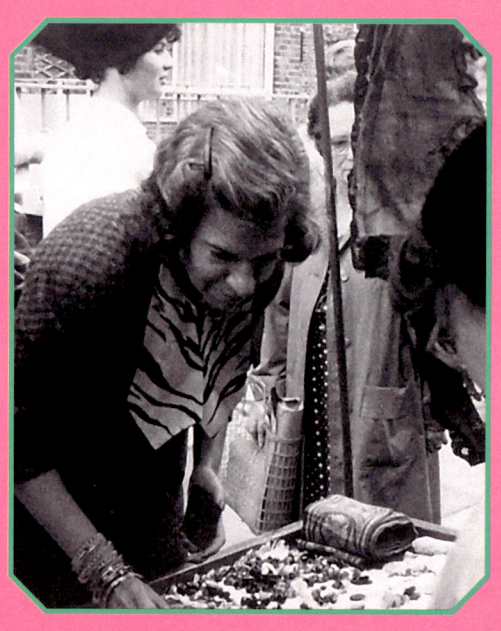

You could get me up at three in the morning and I'd be groggy as hell, but I'd get up and go and hunt for treasure. I get into a store and I'm so *'up'*. When I might not feel so well, it lifts me. It's the whole mechanism of finding the object that I enjoy. It's about spotting the hidden gem.

The first piece I ever bought was in Greenwich Village. I was about 11 or 12 years old, and I had become enchanted by antique shops. Nothing made me happier than foraging around. I found this little shop in the basement of one of those old-fashioned tenement houses that had the fire escapes outside. I'll never forget that place because I thought it was Aladdin's cave. There was this courtly little gentleman, Mr D'Aras, and he was threadbare but always elegant. He had these little pince-nez and wore spats and a monocle. I think I amused him no end. He always greeted me like a mini duchess and encouraged my poking about. I don't think he'd ever seen a kid be so interested in all this junk before, and he was very kind. I fixed on this lacy

↓ RING A DING DING

brooch with rhinestones in it; I just thought it was the cat's pyjamas, and I really lusted after that piece. I didn't have a penny but I saved and saved. I bought it for the magnificent sum of 65 cents. I was so thrilled.

Some of my things are antiques, some are vintage, some are new. I'm drawn to anything that's beautiful, it doesn't matter what it's made from. I'm not drawn to one era. Style is not about expense. I think the best-dressed people are often the ones who have to make do, who have to be inventive. That was so true of Europe after the Second World War.

Dressing up creatively can make an ordinary moment a stellar occasion.

It's sad when people who are drawn to unusual things don't know where to find them, or don't have the confidence to pick them out. My collection is a very personal one. I've built it slowly over many years. I didn't buy it to impress anyone, I bought everything because I liked it, and every piece has a story behind it.

When I didn't know any better and we first went to Paris, years and years ago right after the war, the antique dealers would say, *'You must come early in the morning.'* You'd have to get there at 4.20am with a searchlight, and it was always damp and cold and miserable. We did that for a while and then Carl ♡ said to me,

'This is really stupid, you don't buy what other people buy. Almost everything you buy, you always say, "It has to have my name on it." If it's got your name on it baby, it's gonna be here at 11 o'clock in the morning.'

So that's what we did from then on – and he was right.

→   IF YOU HAVE TO WEAR GLASSES...

← READY TO ROLL

EVERYTHING HAS AN INFLUENCE

I'd rather be at a flea market than almost any place. I'm sad that so many have disappeared. I've always been intrigued by them. I used to go all the time when we went to London.

I started collecting spectacle frames when I was a little girl, so every time I saw a pair at a flea market I would pick them up – they were so cheap in those days. I didn't even need them then, but I thought they were a wonderful accessory.

↑   HUNTING FLEA-MARKET TREASURES, PARIS

Now I have more pairs than I could count – and the bigger and brighter, the better.

If I am going to wear glasses ... then I am going to wear glasses. They have to have some heft.

Wear things that say, this is me,

 WHAT'S NEW PUSSYCAT?

Some of my Zenni collection. Pussycat was a pet-name for the love of my life, my husband Carl ♡. He loved a pair of statement glasses as much as I did. And always wore them well. This cerulean pair were inspired by him.

this is who I am.

There's inspiration everywhere if you choose to look.

I get inspired often just by breathing! To be honest, I am a mirror. I'm simply sensitive to my surroundings. But I don't copy. Sometimes you put all kinds of different things together and it looks like they were born to be that way. I love that. I compile ideas to tell a new story.

Everything

has a story.

EVERYTHING HAS AN INFLUENCE

FROM FRIEND AND DESIGNER

Tommy Hilfiger

Iris is a force of nature. She's not only a fashion icon, but a fashion creator. She understands colours and fabrics better than anyone else. I know that the way she lives her life and puts herself together inspires people from all walks of life. She is a colourful character, who inspires creatives in the fashion and art world. She teaches all of us every time we have the opportunity to connect with her.

2
I LIKE HAPPY COLOURS

On the power of colour

FOR ZENNI OPTICAL
RUVÉN AFANADOR
2021

Emerald green is the dream.

I'm all about colour. I have always gravitated towards colourful things. I have never been a 'neutral' person. I'm not a pastel person either. Pastels make me nervous.

I could never be like my mother, because she never had a hair out of place. She got up in the morning and she looked like she just stepped out of a Chicago Coin Band Box. She was a working gal, but she was glamorous.

She was perfect all the time, very ladylike and elegant. And I'm not like that. As a messy teenager it drove me mad.

Everybody would turn around to look at her, but in a completely different way to me. My mother was much more disciplined in that way than I am, but I learned early on that I have to be my own person to be content.

When I think of my mother, and how she decorated the apartment, I think of colours like warm browns and deep reds, leafy greens: the colours of autumn.

But she would love my use of bright colours, and would say, *'That's my girl'*. My father was, I would say, a typical man of that time. When I think of my father, I don't remember his colours. He paid no attention to what he wore, but funnily enough he always looked marvellous – he had a natural sense of style. He had to be lassoed into dressing up, and when he did, the ladies noticed. But he only had eyes for Mother.

← **MA AND PA**
Dressed to the nines, 1930s, and with friends, 1970s (ma is far right, a vision in orange).

Carl ♡

He was like sunshine.

My husband loved colour on me and colour on him. He was colourful head to toe – neckties, socks, you name it, he wore it.

I always say I like happy colours. I don't remember having one favourite colour as a kid; I just loved colour, period. Little Iris liked the same colours as Big Iris does today.

Little Iris is still around. She's my inner child, I listen to her.

You bring us many happy hours. Your smile, your stare, your baby way

From:— Granma, Ben and Pa

We always agree.

← WHERE ARE THE YEARS GOING?
↓ ASTORIA, NEW YORK, I AM ABOUT 15 YEARS OLD

FOR *Harper's Bazaar Arabia*
RICHARD PHIBBS
2021

What is a happy colour? It's all about tonality – clear, pure and bright tones of colour are what I surround myself with. I have always said I never met a colour I didn't like, but there are tones that I dislike – nothing murky or muddy, thank you. I avoid them because they don't feel powerful to me. They don't suit me. They don't give me energy.

The brighter the better. That's where the energy lies. Gemstone colours all the way.

I even wore a pink wedding dress. It was strapless, lace, fitted with a full skirt and had a little cape with it. I sketched it and a couturier my mother knew made it. I'm really very practical, so I wanted something I could wear afterwards for formal occasions and not just put in storage. I still have my matching pale-pink satin shoes. I'm a big believer in investment pieces – good clothes last forever. If you hang around long enough, everything comes back in style.

Let's face it, life can be dull; you might as well have a little fun with colour when you dress.

→ CARL ♡, DRESSED AS SUNSHINE

Black, on its own, makes me feel kind of drab. I used to go uptown to Harlem on Sundays when I was a kid and watch all the ladies going to church. They had real style. It was a spectacle. You don't see that sort of style much anymore.

But black … when I wear it combined with one of my happy colours … pop! It is transformed, and I feel chic, confident. My mother always said that if you have a good simple little black dress, you'll always have something to wear, and if you have different accessories, you can have 27 outfits.

When life feels bland, try a sudden colour pop.

I particularly like black with its most contrasting pairing: pure white. I'm very partial to it. Black and white together are extremely elegant – timeless, of course. Confidence and clarity, for all occasions.

I put colours together because it makes me feel good.

IRIS APFEL

FOR *L'Officiel Paris*
JEREMY LIEBMAN
2016

Radiant violet with canary yellow or lime green, a vivid blue turquoise with sunset orange, or Chinese red and emerald green. They make me feel better, always. They give me the impetus to do things I might not otherwise do. Like get out of bed. These colours exude humour to me.

Sometimes the most thrilling thing in the world is a technicolour feast.

I'll never forget, I woke up on the morning of my 100th birthday to find that the two lovely girls who were taking care of me had transformed the apartment with hundreds of balloons carpeting the place – all beautiful, bright colours like a jar of jellybeans. It was like walking in a magical balloon forest. It was quite the colour rush.

Bright, bold and fun,

FOR *Evening Standard*
THOMAS WHITESIDE
2012

yum
yum.

I LIKE HAPPY COLOURS

Colour is powerful because it is very emotional.

Courage is red. My favourite shade of lipstick is very, very, bright, bright, bright red, with hot pink second. Bright red lipstick is the perfect combination of minimal elegance and maximal impact. Or as Man Ray put it,

'The dash and dignity of a courageous heart.'

I love that.

But it can't be just any red. I like all the ones that go towards the orangey palette – sunset orange. I love it. It's a *'yes'* colour. It perks me up in a way that blue-reds don't.

One of my first big fashion purchases was an orangey-red Lanvin coat with a big cockade that I bought, along with a black satin cape, at one of the *cabines* in Paris. I blush to recount the price – it was so different in those days. We were soon to be leaving Paris, but they arranged to deliver my purchases to the ship. *'Aucun problème, Madame,'* the charming *vendeuse* said. *'They will be in your state room when you arrive in Cannes.'* And they were, trussed up in a gorgeous box tied with silk ribbons. What a thrill!

I LIKE HAPPY COLOURS

Bright red and turquoise are the colours of adventure. I feel adventurous with them. Millicent Rogers had a huge, heavy necklace in her collection made of irregular chunks of turquoise. It knocked my socks off, it was pure dynamite! Mainly I wear turquoise because it reminds me of many things in my life – those holiday years with Carl ♡ – and it makes me feel alive. Sometimes I wear all turquoise.

FOR ZENNI OPTICAL
RUVÉN AFANADOR
2021

There was a beautiful turquoise and green suit in my collection for H&M, in a divine jacquard fabric with embroidery and lovely little pearl peas. I loved it. When you put it on, it felt like you were in haute couture. And I put it with a fantastic orange and green necklace with an emerald-green frog pendant that you could pop out and wear as a brooch. It was a little bit wild, but versatile. Emerald green is a colour I feel good in.

↓ WEARING MY H&M SUIT, NEW YORK, 2021

FOR *Harper's Bazaar Arabia*
RICHARD PHIBBS
2021

Patience is teal blue. Calm is a soft blue – looking out to the ocean, looking up to the sky as the sun sets and rises.

Denim blue is the colour of determination. At least it was for me. I'm probably one of the first women in America to wear blue jeans. I was wholly dedicated to the pursuit of indigo. I adore jeans. I have so many pairs. They're a canvas for creativity.

Violet is the colour of holidays, flowers, and also goodbyes ...

The weather is fine Beautiful Sunset Cool Breezes,

↓ WITH CARL, LIFE WAS A HOLIDAY

← ESTÉE LAUDER'S HOUSE, PALM BEACH
Designed in 1930 by Howard Major it was built in the Louis XVI style.

I'm crazy for a big hat. The photo overleaf was taken in Capri. Capri was wonderful. It was, for many years, the epicentre of our Mediterranean meanderings. I had a lot of clothes made there. I found a great dressmaker on a street near to our hotel, the Grand Hotel Quisisana. (Quisisana means: *'here lies health'*.)

I love putting green and pink together. The combination makes me want to go dancing. Pink lipstick makes me want to give everyone a kiss!

What makes you feel alive?

Where did I get my style? It came along with me and it grew like topsy. It evolved. I don't differentiate between dressing a body and dressing a space.

If you love wearing a colour, why not live with it too?

The way I dress may be *'different'* or *'eccentric'* to some, but I don't dress to be stared at; I dress for myself. Controlled baroque, that's me. I've always liked things that look old. Makes me look better. But I like to mix high and low, putting things together to wear as the spirit moves me. You have to be true to yourself. Beyond that, there's really no method.

When you try too hard, you look uncomfortable, like you're wearing a costume. If that's happening, I say abandon the whole thing. Once you take it too seriously, it's a curse. It's better to be happy than well dressed and not yourself. Who wants to look in the mirror and see someone else?

I get asked, *'What is the most important thing about an outfit?'* and I believe it's the person inside it.

↑   CAN A HAT EVER BE TOO BIG?

I LIKE HAPPY COLOURS

Sometimes I dress in a more romantic, softer way. Like mellow jazz. Sometimes I dress with a sharp edge. Sometimes I dress just how I'm feeling. You may have noticed, that I'm not a minimalist. More is more and less is a bore, always.

Wear whatever you damn well please! Remember, when you don't dress like everyone else, you don't have to think like everyone else.

FOR *Harper's Bazaar Russia*
CHRISTOPHER STURMAN
2010

I actually like clothes that are architectural and basic, and extreme cuts – but the complete look has got to be big and bold and have lots of pizazz. It's a tangible expression of how I feel about things. A bit of daring, a bit of zip. That's where the pops of colour and my accessories come in. As much as people say they don't want to be bothered, being dressed up always makes someone feel better.

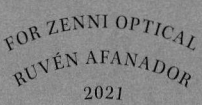

FOR ZENNI OPTICAL
RUVÉN AFANADOR
2021

I'm a hopeless romantic as far as shopping's concerned. The colours and the patterns speak to me.

Carl ♡ used to say I look at a piece of fabric and listen to the threads. It tells me a story. It sings me a song. If I don't get that physical reaction to something, I don't buy it. It's a coup de foudre, a bolt of lightning. It's fun to get knocked out that way!

If you apply that idea, through your choice of accessories, you can make anything individual and make it your own. That's advice from the depths of the Depression, but it still applies today.

We travelled about, Carl ♡ and I, to find the mills that could weave our fabrics, and travelling gave me a great opportunity to find things. I went twice a year to Europe. The offices of the mills were in Paris, and I was always there around couture time, so we got to know France pretty well.

Travel made my life a colourful tapestry.

I liked every place I went. Istanbul is very dear to me … a colour *'eureka'* moment! And not just the lively colours of the buzzing Grand Bazaar, which was indescribably exciting with all the warm spice shades and the fabulous clothing. I remember sailing up the Bosphorus and into Istanbul for the first time with my father under an azure-blue sky. I remember one of the early years with Carl ♡, when we came in on a spring morning, on the boat from a port in western Italy, and swam in the clear, crisp-blue waters with dolphins playing along beside us. I was obsessed with the glowing gold-coloured tins they gave you for your soap and wash cloth at the baths in Bursa, where the Turkish towel came from. I kept my tin and still use it as a handbag.

London never failed to knock me out. Hong Kong. Berlin. Ireland, which was so charming – we sailed there to go antiquing in 1958. Amsterdam – those floating flower markets! I can still see the greenery of Barcelona, down all the little winding streets, and all the silver jewellery. And of course Antoni Gaudí's colours everywhere. My fellow lover of colour and all things unusual.

I found Mexico City spectacular for many reasons, especially the architecture – but I was staggered

by Frida Kahlo and Diego Rivera's homestead. It was like a dream, in a colour palette like no other. Those saturated colours, all the bright, bold brilliance.

We covered every square inch of Italy over the years, and we'd get the boat from there to North Africa. So many adventures, from Caserta, to Venice, to Milan and Capri. Every alleyway filled with vibrant buttons and the palest lace. I think of little plates of bursting ripe-red tomatoes in Roman trattorias, and the courtyard filled with orange trees in the grand Doria Pamphilj Palace. The crisp-white cotton aprons and black-olive eyes of the little boys who served the espresso in Naples' coffee bars. Venice's Moorish architecture and the peeling paint on the striped pylons and the pageantry in Siena around Il Palio, the medieval race in the Piazza del Campo. Italy was very special to us.

But I fell madly in love with North Africa and the Middle East. Being in these parts of the world awakened my senses and stirred something in my bones. I think I was born with a *'souk sense'*. Beirut and Tunis were enchanting, as exciting as Paris, which at the time was considered by us Americans as the most elegant city in the world. I loved them.

I remember Naples and my feeling of surprise at it being as busy, boisterous and bold, and as much of a melting-pot of ideas for me, as the cities I had fallen for in North Africa. I like any place where I can forage about; the energy and excitement of the unexpected, not knowing what I'm going to find. My dream journey would still be from souk to souk, from North Africa to the Middle East. The colours in those places are so sophisticated, and I have always gravitated towards colourful things.

I think the most colourful place I've ever been to is Tangier. I vividly remember coming off the boat and seeing the bright colour of the trees for the first time. Bright colours, bright, friendly people, lots of parties, gold and white dresses. It was a rich experience.

Wherever we wandered, Carl ♡ and I, we had a habit of walking into colourful scenes. On one visit to Sidi Bou Said, a tiny town perched on a cliffside outside Tunis, we were lucky enough to be invited to the wedding of the mayor's daughter in the town square. It was late at night and the whole village seemed to be there. I loved that town – it was a bit like a miniature Capri. All the houses were white with azure doors and woodwork, and it's all cobblestone streets filled with flowers.

Another time we were pulled into a lunch under the cypress trees in Crete when we admired the grapes drying on an embankment, and in rural Ireland we were asked in for tea by a wonderful antique fire when we stopped to ask an elderly gentleman if we could photograph his beautiful fat thatched roof. I was invited as a guest of honour to a banquet held the night before the Palio in Siena. Another time, when we stopped to admire the white wedding horse covered with silver for a rural wedding procession in Morocco, we were duly invited to the wedding party.

We didn't speak the language

FROM FRIEND AND PHOTOGRAPHER

Ruvén Afanador

When I began my photography career, I saw the world in black and white. The absence of colour created drama and mystery, and served as an homage to my favourite images created by Penn, Avedon and Chambi. Over time and during my many trips to Mexico, India and South America, I started to look at colour differently. I searched for ways to translate my black and white language into colour. It was during this search that I first became aware of Iris Apfel. Her fearlessness with colour both intrigued and impressed me. Like a great symphony conductor, she mixed unexpected colour palettes with tone on tone layering to create her own unique rainbow. Years later, I photographed Iris for the first of many times, and found myself lucky to observe her as she styled clothing and accessories for our photos. Her instinctive decisions showed an inherent level of sophistication, confidence and taste only acquired from living a life of style and beauty. It has been an honour to know and to learn from Iris. I now look at the use of colour in my own photography as an homage to Iris.

3
NEVER STOP BEING BOLD

On playfulness

FOR *Süddeutsche Zeitung*
ANDREAS LASZLO
2011

If life is a party, it's the people that make it. You can have a spectacular setting and wonderful food and all those things, but if the company isn't fun, it's nothing. People who are curious and who have a sense of humour make the best friends. I think those are the two great gifts that I got in my cradle – I really believe that – and I seek out people who have them too.

Laugh as often as you can! It's a blessing.

I want everybody to have a good time. I love to make people laugh, it makes me very happy. I seek happiness. I just try to get a kick out of things, whenever possible. I guess that's why I love happy colours.

It's so easy to amuse me. I want to find the fun and humour in everything.

Intelligent fun, that is – I never believed in chasing pleasure (caviar was always my drug of choice, yum yum – we gave it up when Carl ♡ went on a low-salt diet and sometimes I still dream of it).

I really believe there would be a lot less cruelty and coldness in the world if more people remembered what it was like to be a child, and listened to that inner child.

It's important to keep that part of you alive. You see things differently.

I don't feel childish, I feel childlike. Big difference.

My husband Carl ♡ was the same way. Lucky we found each other! I met Carl ♡ up at Lake George. A friend and I had saved our money, and it was the first time I was able to pay for my own holiday from my first job. Carl ♡ told my friend he thought I would be very attractive if I went and had my nose fixed. I said, *'You can tell him where to go. This is the way I come.'*

Despite his critique, he asked my friend for my particulars and how to reach me when we got back to New York. A few weeks passed and I came home from work one day to the phone ringing off the hook – it was Carl ♡. He said,

'I love that outfit you wore today.'

He told me that he loved my hat and that I had on a smashing suit. I said, *'My goodness, were you in my closet?'*

He happened to be on Fifth Avenue coming back from a business appointment when the bus he was riding broke down right in front of Bonwit Teller, a big store where Trump Towers is now. While he was sitting on the bus waiting for someone to come and fix it, I was standing there with my mother and my old beau, Arthur Englander – a buyer of haute couture for Neiman Marcus in Dallas, who was crazy about my mother and used to stay at her apartment when he came to New York. We'd been to lunch at the Plaza Hotel with her, and he wanted to walk me back to my job, but as we passed Bonwit Teller, he and my mother stopped to discuss the outfits in the window display.

Carl♡ asked me for a date. I said no – this was September. I had a lot of boyfriends, and I never wanted to get married. I was having too much fun. Every time he asked me for a date I was busy. The first opportunity for me to see Carl♡ was the evening of Columbus Day, in October. My roommate was getting married that day, but I was free in the evening.

My roommate had a very charming gentleman friend whom she had wanted me to meet for months and months. I had refused to meet him, because I never went on blind dates, but we finally met at her wedding. He invited me for dinner afterwards, but I told him that I already had a dinner date for 6pm at the Waldorf Astoria, which was right across the street from the wedding. All afternoon he told me I had to break that date.

Finally, to shut him up, I agreed to go for dinner with him. I agreed to stand up Carl♡. I couldn't reach Carl♡ to cancel – there were no mobile phones at the time. But when the clock struck 6pm, I found that I just couldn't do it.

I ran across the street to meet Carl ♡, and I'm so grateful that I did. He was funny and cool and charming and cuddly and he cooked Chinese food. I couldn't do any better.

Sometimes, it's all down to good timing.

On Thanksgiving, Carl ♡ proposed. Christmas I got blinged. On Washington's birthday, we were married at the Waldorf Astoria. I never wanted a wedding; I wanted to elope. I could think of more practical uses for the money. But the parents and the grandparents wanted the wedding. It was fairly small, but very beautiful. We went to Palm Beach for our honeymoon and we lived on holiday ever after.

No matter what age, no matter what gender, love is priceless.

NEVER STOP BEING BOLD

When dear Albert Maysles' documentary came out, people said to me, *'We came expecting a fashion film and instead we got a love story'*. And it was a love story. It was about the two great passions in my life: my work and Carl ♡. I'm considered to be fairly hip for an antique, but when it came to marriage, I was an old-fashioned square. We did almost everything together for 68 years. We even wore the same fragrance. Carl ♡ passed away at the age of 100, just short of 101. He would have been so unhappy about that, I know, because he so wanted to be 101.

Carl ♡ had something special. He just had *'it'*. He was truly a gentleman. He was so gallant and so generous. He was a graduate of the New York University School of Advertising.

He pushed me into the limelight and then basked in my success.

He'd bring his toolbox to my early interior jobs and watch me work, and he was my private paparazzo. What could be luckier than finding someone who cheers for you? When I received praise for something, he got more of a kick from it than I did. And he had a fantastic, crazy sense of humour. He was deliciously funny.

↑   OUR HONEYMOON, PALM BEACH, 1948

We were always carrying around a lot of drapery and upholstery fabrics on our travels, and in all these little towns I'd find a local dressmaker, make sketches, and over time I developed a wardrobe. After some time, I thought, well, this isn't fair on Carl ♡. I decided to take the wildest fabric we had and have a pair of trousers made for him. Everyone would say, *'Carl, those pants are sensational!'* They'd ask him where he got them from, and he would reply,

'I just shot my couch.'

There were many pairs after that – some were wacky, others more elegant, but he wore them all proudly.

He often went along with other fun stuff too: hats, you name it. I bought a ring for him in Dublin sometime in the fifties – I convinced the dealer to sell it to me right off his own finger – and Carl ♡ never took it off. The only place we ever had our differences was in the flea markets.

We never stopped having fun. I think you need to be patient and have a sense of humour in a marriage. I don't think you want to smother anyone, or be jealous – that's very important. My husband always gave me all the space I needed, including in the closet.

But even that he took in good humour. I remember when Harold Koda – who was then the curator in charge at the Costume Institute of the Metropolitan Museum of Art – and his team came to our apartment to choose outfits for my show, clothing seemed to gush in every direction.

We had to move all the furniture in the apartment aside, and Carl ♡ announced with a big smile that he could sleep in a drawer.

In the early days of our business we'd be lugging around a suitcase full of samples that was so heavy, Carl ♡ couldn't carry it. He put wheels on it and I used to joke that if he'd stuck with that invention we'd have been made for the rest of our lives. He'd say,

'But think of all the fun we would have missed.'

That's just who he was.

My philosophy is to live in the now – yesterday is gone, you don't know if there's even going to be a tomorrow, so you might as well enjoy today.

As my husband used to say,

You should really live every day as if it were your last, because one day you'll be right.

You have to make your own fun. Why not amuse people? I think people should indulge in a little bit of creativity ... it's a chance for them to play.

I think too many people get themselves into such a snit about what to wear or what not to wear.

Dressing up should be fun.

Dress exactly the way you want to and you'll always look wonderful, because you'll feel wonderful – you'll feel like yourself.

You have to look in the mirror and see yourself and not somebody else.

The world has got a lot more homogenised, and I think fashion is a mirror of society. In New York, you can sometimes tell a person's zip code by what they're wearing. I'm always on the lookout for originals; I'm like Diogenes with the lantern. I would love to bring back a *'trendless'* world, where there's no such thing as *'in'* or *'out'*. In my nineties, I was still wearing a beautiful black Norman Norell dress that I wore when I had my first date with my husband. We've all got a personality, and I think people should exploit that, and not try to hide it. My closet is full of joy. It should be about joy.

For me, it's the fun of the process that I like more than anything.

If I've got someplace to be, I'll spend more time getting dressed than I'll spend at the actual event. I love to dig around and find things in my own closet that surprise me.

But sometimes I wear what I had on the day before, too, because it's all put together already, and I can just jump into it, jump on my broom and fly off! And that's fine too.

Laugh. If you can keep a sense of humour, and stay childlike, you will be open to new people and things, and you'll always be ready for adventures.

A smile a day keeps the doctor away.

I LOVE …

A good joke.

Puppies.

Lots of animals. *(People send me pictures of their own pets dressed up in outfits like mine – who wouldn't get a kick out of that?)*

Ornaments.

Stuffed toys, a whole menagerie. They're my guys, I love them.

I'm totally cuckoo for over-the-knee boots: I think they're the greatest.

I love anything with feathers: peacocks, owls, flamingos.

Boas and fun dyed furs. I don't care for serious furs.

And teddy bears.

Something delicious to eat. I always loved truffle pizza from this one place in Palm Beach, most Italian food actually … and grilled cheese.

A good little cake.

And real food at a party – not fancy-schmancy lettuce things.

A little tropical fruit print.

A purse shaped like a dog.

Ladybug bracelets.

And I love things that are sophisticated but actually a little whimsical, a little wacky.

Smoking slippers with a wink on them.

I'm crazy about jazz. Old jazz.

Sabrina and *Some Like It Hot*.

When the people I love are happy.

Saul Steinberg, the artist cartoonist – his work is witty, playful.

Sneakers with sequins.

Holiday decorations all year round.

LOVE, LOVE, LOVE.

A
GOOD
JOKE...

ORNAMENTS...
STUFFED TOYS...
TEDDY BEARS...
BEAUTIFUL BUGS...

SOPHISTICATED
AND WACKY AT
THE SAME TIME...

SPARKLE
AND SEQUINS...

When I started working with the designers at Dr. Scholl's, it was another opportunity to draw on everything I have loved in my life, and reinvent it all again – this time as shoes. How marvellous.

I've always said, if your hair is done properly and you're wearing good shoes, you can get away with anything. I've taken this far in life.

I crave colour. Colour is life. It brightens the spirit. It brightens the soul.

I love shoes that are bold and fun.

↑ DR. SCHOLL'S ICONIC ORIGINAL WOODEN SANDAL

It was the inspiration for this collection, in honour of the brand's 100th anniversary.

The Mr. Carl design reminds me of the slippers he used to wear every day inside our apartment. He was iconic.

↓ REVIEWING DESIGNS FOR THE MR. CARL.

Everything has a story if you look and listen hard enough.

Everything informs everything else, always.

You just got to mix it up. Start with what you know, then create something new.

My creative story started with textiles and continues – one beautiful accessory at a time.

NEVER STOP BEING BOLD

I just adore him. I have a denim shirt with him on it that I've had for years. I like to say I'm the older woman in his life. He's not much younger than I am, but it sounds good, right?

And Kermit too. There was a big ostrich called Gussie in our Palm Beach apartment: you lifted up her wing and her belly was full of booze. Kermit stuck close to her and he became a terrible lush in the process.

I love playful things.

↗ SOME MORE PIECES FROM MY COLLECTION
They all have a story to tell, I am just part of that story.

I have a lot of playful jewellery. I'd honestly get more kick out of a drop-dead discount ring or bangle that cost four dollars than a visit to Harry Winston. I have a strong neck and arms from all the crazy necklaces and bangles – sometimes you have to suffer for your art.

Carl ♡ had a lot of crummy watches along with his fine ones – not that he ever knew what time it was! But they made him happy.

I just don't care about diamonds and I'm not interested in fine jewellery. I think manufacturers and artists are much more creative with costume jewellery, because the materials aren't so expensive, so they can take more chances and do more interesting pieces.

It's all about movement and colour and joy and possibility. Like one of my pins that's all pavé stones. When you look at it, at first it looks like a nineteenth-century dandy with a long frock coat and interesting hat, like a top hat, but it's a trembling piece – its head wiggles. When you look closer, he's not a gentleman, he's a monkey. He's really quite wonderful.

NEVER STOP BEING BOLD

FOR ZENNI OPTICAL
RUVÉN AFANADOR
2021

My home is filled with amusing things.

FOR *Harper's Bazaar Russia*
CHRISTOPHER STURMAN
2010

If you're a serious person, it's good to have a serious house. But I like to have fun with my surroundings. There's a lot of good decorating around, and while some of these homes are very beautiful, they look anonymous to me. They could be expensive hotel suites – you have no sense of the person who lives there. I like a house with a few mistakes, rather than something that's utter perfection.

I think it was Diana Vreeland who said, *'you can suffer from too much good taste'*. I like to be surrounded by things that give me pleasure to look at, but they don't have to belong together in anyone else's eyes. They make sense to me, that's what matters. I always want people to leave my home feeling joyful and relaxed after absorbing some of the humour that I have here – I collect everything that's not nailed down, so I have some cuckoo things – and I always hope that they'll want to come back.

You need to make it up as you go along.

One of the most important things for creativity is the opportunity for improvisation. I remember one of my early interior jobs, with the interior decorator Elinor Johnson, where we needed to find a coffee table for an apartment. This was in the middle of World War Two, and there was no furniture delivery to be had.

I remember going down to the Bowery and finding some old columns. We cut the capitals off them and then, back at the apartment, put a piece of thick glass on top of the capitals. It was a striking piece, a wonderful cocktail table, and it wouldn't have existed without the need to improvise.

Rules leave no room for play.

My first big job in beauty and fashion came when I was the tender age of 90 – when I designed a line of cosmetics for MAC. Nothing in life or art is written in stone. I don't have any rules because I would only be breaking them, so it's a waste of time. I think rules are the ruination of the art world.

Dive into your closets for treasures abound...

You never know what outfits are bound to be found!

Play around with the notes of your ideas and go one way or another, and each time you do it, do it a different way.

A good way to live, don't you think?

NEVER STOP BEING BOLD

OLD WORLD WEAVERS
Silk Fabrics for the Connoisseur
136 E. 57th St., New York, N.Y. 10022, 355-7186-7
Chicago • Dallas • Atlanta • Los Angeles
San Francisco • Seattle • Houston • Denver
Miami • Palm Beach • Washington, D.C.

SOMETIMES YOU HAVE TO MAKE IT UP AS YOU GO ALONG TO GET ANYWHERE.

When I was 20, I transferred from New York University to the University of Wisconsin, and I was missing some credits that I needed in order to fulfil the curriculum. It was a really terrible time for me to find work and figure out how to graduate. There were no classes, and I was going bananas trying to find something I hadn't already studied at NYU. I lost loads of sleep worrying about it.

Lo and behold, one day I came upon two courses – Museum Administrations I and Museum Administrations II. I found the teacher – a little elderly guy – behind a big desk in a building way across campus. He said, *'What can I do for you?'* I said, *'I came here to register for your course.'* And he said, *'Oh my God! You're the first person to do so in nearly a decade.'*

I think he was patiently waiting to retire; he'd given up hope of any students coming his way. Anyway, we started talking and he was charming. I said, *'Well, you must have some idea of what you want to teach and what you want me to do?'* He said he didn't have a clue, so I suggested we figure it out together. Eventually I got out of him that he'd always had a yearning to start a museum dedicated to American culture.

NEVER STOP BEING BOLD

We agreed that I would write a paper on the history of American jazz. I'd been a jazz buff since I was a kid in high school – a whole contingent from my high school in Long Island City used to go each week and see Benny Goodman's band playing during the recording of the NBC programme *Let's Dance*, dancing up a storm in the aisles in our saddle shoes – so I was skipping at the idea of this. I was very happy, only to realise when I got to the library that there was not a single thing there about the history of American jazz – this was 1940 after all. What was I going to do?

I had two weeks' worth of that worry, then I read in the paper that there was something happening at the movie theatre. A piece of good luck! I knew that it was my chance. A long shot, but a chance nonetheless. I cut my classes that afternoon and got dressed up and went to the theatre. I knocked on the theatre door and somebody stuck his head out. His eyes popped as he looked me up and down.

I was in a very preppy outfit: a grey cashmere sweater and flannel trousers, loafers, and a stunning white Cornell blazer – with burgundy piping and fantastic buttons – that an old beau had given me.

He said, *'Lordy, Lordy, who's your tailor? Come on in.'* So I snuck in through the stage door entrance. My great luck was that Duke Ellington, who was the master of jazz, was performing that week in Madison, at the theatre, between movie showings. At the theatre door, I'd met Ray Nance, the violinist in the band. Duke was performing, but Ray said he would introduce me when he came off stage. Duke and I got on famously. I was an enthusiastic student. He said he would do anything he could to help me.

He was one of the most charming men I've ever met, and so elegant and suave.

He regaled me with jazz tales all afternoon. I went back home walking on air. He said I could come back every day – which of course I did. My classroom seat was empty all week. Who could turn down an offer like that? We talked about everything from the style of different musicians to jazz movements. I couldn't believe he gave me his time like that.

At the end of the week, the band were going to Chicago South Side, where there was going to be a kind of meeting of jazz guys in the neighbourhood – a bunch of music greats and friends were stopping by

– and Duke invited me along to meet them all. I'd never imagined anything like it. They were all coming to see Duke play. How could I miss that?

I had neglected to get permission from my mother, however. When I went back to my sorority, I found out that I couldn't go to Chicago without her permission. I called my mother, and she said no way! I told her I had to go, and that my graduation depended on it, but she still said, *'No. You're not going. Period.'*

So I climbed out of the window, and that's how I got over that hurdle.

I took the milk train to Chicago and stayed in a hotel. It was like I had died and gone to heaven. I got all kinds of information, met so many incredible talents who sat in with Duke for jam sessions. I got home in one piece and I was able to write my paper. I did very well. If you set your brain to try to figure something out, you will. The next paper I did was on the history of American women's hats – but nothing came close to the thrill of an impromptu road trip with the jazz greats.

I like to improvise.

I think I always like to do things as though I'm playing jazz... try this, try that.

← **DIVING IN**

My earlier interior-design days, 1930s.

It's more fun. In my very early days of interior design, some clients couldn't handle it. I didn't have any references or work that they could look at, but they were going on the idea that if I could put together exciting little outfits I might be able to wave my wand at their rooms too.

I never drew up designs of what I was planning, I would research everything I could about their taste and their interests and riffed off those things to create an aesthetic. I dove right in. But in the end, most of them had faith in me and gave me carte blanche to do things as I saw fit, to go with the flow. I enjoyed it more that way. It felt more natural.

↓ TUNISIA, 1970S

You have to love what you're doing with your time on this planet. Start with that. It's a matter of how it feels. I don't do anything, I feel it. If something sounds exciting and interesting, I dive in and worry about it later.

If it feels good, I know it's right. I have always operated in this way. I have always trusted my gut – who else could I trust if I can't trust what's mine?

I think you can overthink things. If something's good, don't question it too much. If it ain't broke, don't fix it. Some things I just don't think about. It can ruin things. I think you have to be loose as a goose.

Once you start to look for cut and dried answers, you get cut and dried results.

I'm a free spirit. I like everything to be free.

Trust yourself and take risks. I have never been much of a conformist on any front, and it hasn't hurt me yet, so I think I've been doing something right. Freedom of expression, and actually expressing yourself, is the most important thing, because if you don't, you're all bottled up.

Going with my gut has taken me everywhere. I never imagined, in my wildest dreams, that any of this life would ever happen to me.

But here

I am.

NEVER STOP BEING BOLD

FROM FRIEND AND PHOTOGRAPHER

Bruce Weber

Iris invented some new colours by mix-matching greens from a secret garden. I can't tell you how or what she did, but when she wears these colours, she's blossoming.

4

GET COMFORTABLE OUTSIDE

On courage

FOR *Harper's Bazaar Arabia*
RICHARD PHIBBS
2021

Confidence is a beautiful thing. I'm not afraid of many things. Snakes. Lightning… that one gets me. Usually, the things I can't control. But I haven't really let fear hold me back. Throughout my life I have always tried to take every opportunity that popped by. And since the day, aged eight, that I assumed my *'dying swan'* ballet position – dressed in a lumpy affair fashioned from a bolt of cheesecloth bought by grandma for some future cleaning job – for a bemused photographer (and to my stylish mother's despair), I've tried to do things my way, without fear of judgement. Otherwise, you miss out on all the fun. It's not always easy, but it's empowering.

But taking any leap, whether it's mastering a new skill, starting a new job, or embarking on a new exciting adventure, requires confidence.

People say I inspire them and I give them courage to do things they wouldn't have done before. Maybe people give me high marks for still being around.

Nothing just happens.

Everything has to be polished.

Or I because I speak the truth and I tell people what I think, which is unusual. Perhaps, through me, they can see that there's a life after 30, and that makes me happy! But when women tell me I've inspired them to go into business or change their professions, to do things they were afraid of, I want to shake them and say, *'Don't wait for someone to give you courage; you can do whatever you damn well please!'*

People are born with the ability to have confidence in themselves. My dad cared not a fig about outside approval and had the courage of his convictions. It's not easy, but it can be worked on too. Self-expression is painful because you have to think about yourself very deeply. And you find out who you are and how you can improve yourself.

We all have bad days. Moments when things don't feel right. It's very uncomfortable when things don't feel right. Get comfortable with that.

Style is a good example. To me, style implies originality, but also courage.

You can't just let it sit there. It takes a lot of hard work. First, you have to find yourself. You have to know who you are and then work at it. Style is a matter of attitude, but you have to possess individuality to have an attitude. You must know who you are and stick to it. You'll find it's hard work at the beginning, but it pays off. People should celebrate their originality and not want to be part of a herd.

You have to study yourself and learn who you are, what you like, what you don't like, what you're comfortable with, what you feel, how people react to you, and how much it bothers you. I never tried to fit in.

If you have to be all things to all people, you end up being nothin' to nobody.

It's a matter of balance, like everything else in life. That takes work to learn. Nothing just happens on its own.

You do have to make a point of getting along with people. If you don't try to be part of things, your originality is going to work against you. When you have the trust of others, then they tend to embrace you when you do something original. There is a difference between being perceived as original and being accepted – even loved – for it, and being perceived as different and resented for it.

Doing new things takes a lot of strength. A lot of energy. It can be very tiring trying to make things happen, to push fears aside. It's much easier to go with the flow – that's what most people do. But it's not very interesting.

FOR ZENNI OPTICAL
RUVÉN AFANADOR
2021

You only fail if you don't try.

GET COMFORTABLE

When I think of my own grandmother and grandfather and what they came through, I realise they had no choice but to push fears aside. They were 15 and 16 when they got married, and they had a traditional wedding in Russia. Shortly thereafter, my grandfather got his papers saying that he had to join the Russian army, which he did not want to do. The only way out was to run away, and that's what he decided to do. He went to America.

← MY GRANDPARENTS: GUMPTION

He had hardly been married to Grandma, and she was pregnant, but he had to go. He went, and he told her that as soon as he got to America and made money, he would send her a ticket. Can you imagine, as a teenage girl, being in such a condition? I mean, the average girl would be a nervous wreck. She hardly knew him. Would he send the ticket? He was very honourable, but I don't know how she lived without going with him.

At a party one night, a man came on horseback with a letter, and the letter was from Grandpa. He had made and saved money, and now it was time for Grandma to come and join him. Wow. She had never left the state and spoke only Russian, yet she had to travel a huge distance with a four-month-old baby (my mother), all the way to Germany, then wait in Hamburg for the ship to come. Unfortunately, the ship was late, so she had to use some of the money Grandpa had given her earlier than expected.

Can you imagine travelling that far? And this was the nineteenth century. Not knowing a single soul, not knowing the language? Grandma was a remarkable woman.

← MY GRANDFATHER, THE MASTER TAILOR

You are the best Grandma in the world.

Finally, the ship came and they got on it, but it was a very rough voyage. Everybody was sick and it took a long time to get there. I can understand why, years later, she still never wanted to go on a ship again.

My grandparents were reunited and settled in a tenement walk-up apartment on the umpteenth floor in New York City. My grandma set about making and sewing and cleaning – she used up all the housewifely genes in one generation, Mama and I received nary a one. My grandfather was a master tailor. It was fabulous, old-world, high-end tailoring. He had a lot of style, and he worked like a horse. He thought America was the greatest thing that ever happened, and it was. He worked hard to make money to buy tickets for the whole family and sent for them.

But he got sick in the process. The doctor said, you will have an old age, but if you want to have a good old age, you better get out of the city, away from all the frenzy of this life, and seek the seclusion and fresh air of the countryside. The countryside at the time was Queens, so that's what they did.

There was no bridge, so they had to find a boatman, pack up their belongings and travel across the water to the pastoral shores of Queensboro.

It was quite a trip. They landed in Long Island City and became early settlers of the area, on a little farm with one goat and part-ownership of a cow. Grandma kept a kosher home. There were no stores in Long Island City, much less a kosher store. So once a week, they had to get up at four in the morning and walk to the rail station. There was a one-way train. It was very primitive. Then they had to walk to the water's edge and wait for the ferry to come. They had to get on the ferry and go across the East River, then take a horsecar down to the Lower East Side, spend all day shopping for provisions, and come back late at night. The bridge to Manhattan wasn't built until 1910. They wouldn't get back until midnight or close to midnight, with everything for the week.

Even though I'm a New Yorker through and through (since Carl ♡ and I married I lived in the city), I grew up out there, in Astoria, the residential section of Long Island

↓ WITH MY GRANDPA

City on the edge of the East River, on a kind of *'compound'* with my mother's family. We could see the bright lights of Manhattan from there.

I was the first grandchild on both sides of the family for some years. When I was a little girl, when we visited my father's parents' home in Brooklyn for a family gathering, for the first 15 minutes all the aunts and uncles would dote on me and pinch my cheek and talk to me, then they'd go off and have a drink and play cards or something like that. I must have been about five years old, and I needed something to do. My grandmother led me by the hand to the back hallway where there were two big closets full of what looked like pillowcases tied in knots. She opened two of the pillowcases and started to spill little bits of fabrics of all kinds, of all shapes and sizes, out onto the floor, and my eyes popped. She said,

'Look, you can play with all these scraps – just play and do whatever you want with them.'

She collected the pieces for charity sewing projects – she was a very kind woman who did a lot for less fortunate people, and her four daughters worked on the sewing too. She helped to establish a hospital and an old folks' home … quite remarkable. Anyway, she sometimes let me choose some of her fabric scraps to keep. I was already obsessed with texture, colour and pattern, so I spent whole evenings playing with the scraps, arranging them all different ways. It was so exciting for me to put colours together, and time flew. I never wanted to go home when the time came. It was my first experience of how it feels to be creative. My grandmother did that for me. I spent hours and hours at it; it must have honed my eye.

It gave me a very deep interest in fabric, and it opened the door to a life in the textile world – even though I didn't know it at the time. Later, when I wanted to start a fabric business, I just went ahead and figured out how to do it. It didn't occur to me that I couldn't do something just because I was a woman. If I had thought about opening Old World Weavers too much, I probably wouldn't have pursued that dream.

Having courage in your convictions means not worrying what people think. Why would you want to live in someone else's image of what you should be? There were two exceptions. My mother and my husband. If they really hated something I was wearing, for instance, I would change. But as a general rule, I never cared too much. I don't want to offend anybody, but if people don't like something I'm wearing, I feel like that's their thing.

People worry too much about being liked. They think it's the only way to get on in life. You should work at being nice rather than being liked.

If you're true to yourself, the one can lead to the other. Humour got me a long way in Italy. When we first visited a mill there we had to hire an interpreter, because the man in charge spoke no English, and we didn't speak a word of Italian. The interpreter was a funny character with very small eyeglasses. He had a cucumber in his top pocket. Every time he thought our backs were turned he took a bite of it. (I loathe cucumber – maybe someone told him to keep it to himself!)

Who knows what that was about! Anyway, he licked his finger to turn the pages of a dictionary, but the words we needed weren't there. The language of fabric was not there. It turned out we could get by, because we were on the same wavelength as the mill owner and we all understood fabric. But we had to dive in.

Over the years I learned by listening intently. There was no time to go back to school, so I read children's books and tried to piece together words and actions. I had to keep a sense of humour about communicating, and people got a sense of what I meant from my body language and expressions too. When people asked me if I spoke Italian I'd say, *'Yes, with courage and no verbs.'* I developed a huge vocabulary over time, but knew no grammar at all. And I could only speak in the present tense. But it wasn't about speaking it well, it was about making the effort.

I always say if you're gonna do your own thing, first you've got to have a thing to do. That gives you confidence in your convictions. For instance, my vision of an outfit that required blue jeans. It took me about six weeks of hard work.

I got there in the end, but I had a helluva fight on my hands.

Women didn't wear jeans. They couldn't buy jeans. They weren't a fashion item in the late 1930s and early 1940s. I was met with confusion and a hint of dismay when I asked for them at the army-navy store in Wisconsin, where I was at college. But I had this big gingham turban and big earrings that I felt would be perfect with a crisp shirt and work jeans, and I was like a dog with a bone. I'm often like that when I want something.

The shopkeeper said, *'Don't you know, young ladies do not wear jeans. What's wrong with you?'* I said, *'I want a pair; I need a pair.'* Not only would they not size a pair down for me, they almost threw me out. I went back again and again, determined. Every week. Finally, the shopkeeper called me to say that he'd ordered a pair of boys' jeans by mail order. He probably just wanted me off his back at that point. I'm not surprised he was sick of me. Maybe he pitied me. Anyway, I was delirious that they fit me and that the outfit was just as smashing as I had imagined.

I still wear men's jeans; they fit me better. They became my thing. If I had been set back by the first response, it just never would have happened.

I know that's just denim, but it's all part of the same thing.

↑ I LOVE A TURBAN!
Especially paired with jeans.

GET COMFORTABLE   207

Sometimes you just have to take action, even if it is a small step.

I have applied this philosophy to living and it has never steered me wrong.

FROM FRIEND AND DESIGNER

Alexis Bittar

Iris embodies a symphony of colour. Effortlessly, she is fearless about how she lives her life, the ultimate disruptor. In her style sense, she blasts ageism by wearing exactly what she wants, layering colours, genres, patterns. Her daily actions are defiant towards what is expected towards ageing. She is shocking pink, bright red, beaming yellow. She's a symphony. Iris is like a beaming flag of bright colours.

5

YOU ONLY HAVE ONE TRIP.

On longevity

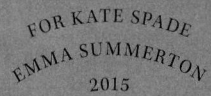

FOR KATE SPADE
EMMA SUMMERTON
2015

As you get older, you worry about different things. When I have a lot of commitments, I do sometimes worry about whether I'm going to get everything done on time. And it's natural to think about matters of health. But I tend to forget the unpleasant things, the sad things. I have a few regrets, but there's no point dwelling on them. I've worked very hard and I've tried my best. I haven't done everything properly and I don't think I know everything. If I make a mistake, I try to correct it and I move on.

I live in the now. If you make a federal case out of everything, you're going to end up a wreck.

You can't live in the past, because that's gone, and you can't bring it back. It's finished – go on to the next mistake. That's just the way I am.

I guess it's funny, then, that I love saloon songs so much. Sad, unrequited love songs. I think they're wonderful – especially Sinatra's, and any rendition of 'Lush Life' (which was written by a young pianist called Billy Strayhorn for Duke Ellington). But that's the limit of my wallowing!

I had a beautiful marriage for 68 years. When Carl ♡ died, I was crushed. I still miss him madly. I didn't think I could manage at first, but I eventually realised he wouldn't want me to sit around, moping. I decided I wouldn't stay home and cry all day.

Carl ♡ really pushed me. All our lives he pushed me, like a stage mother. When opportunities came up and I said, *'Forget it'*, he'd say:

'You've got to do it.'

So, I do. I've worked harder than I ever have in my life ever since.

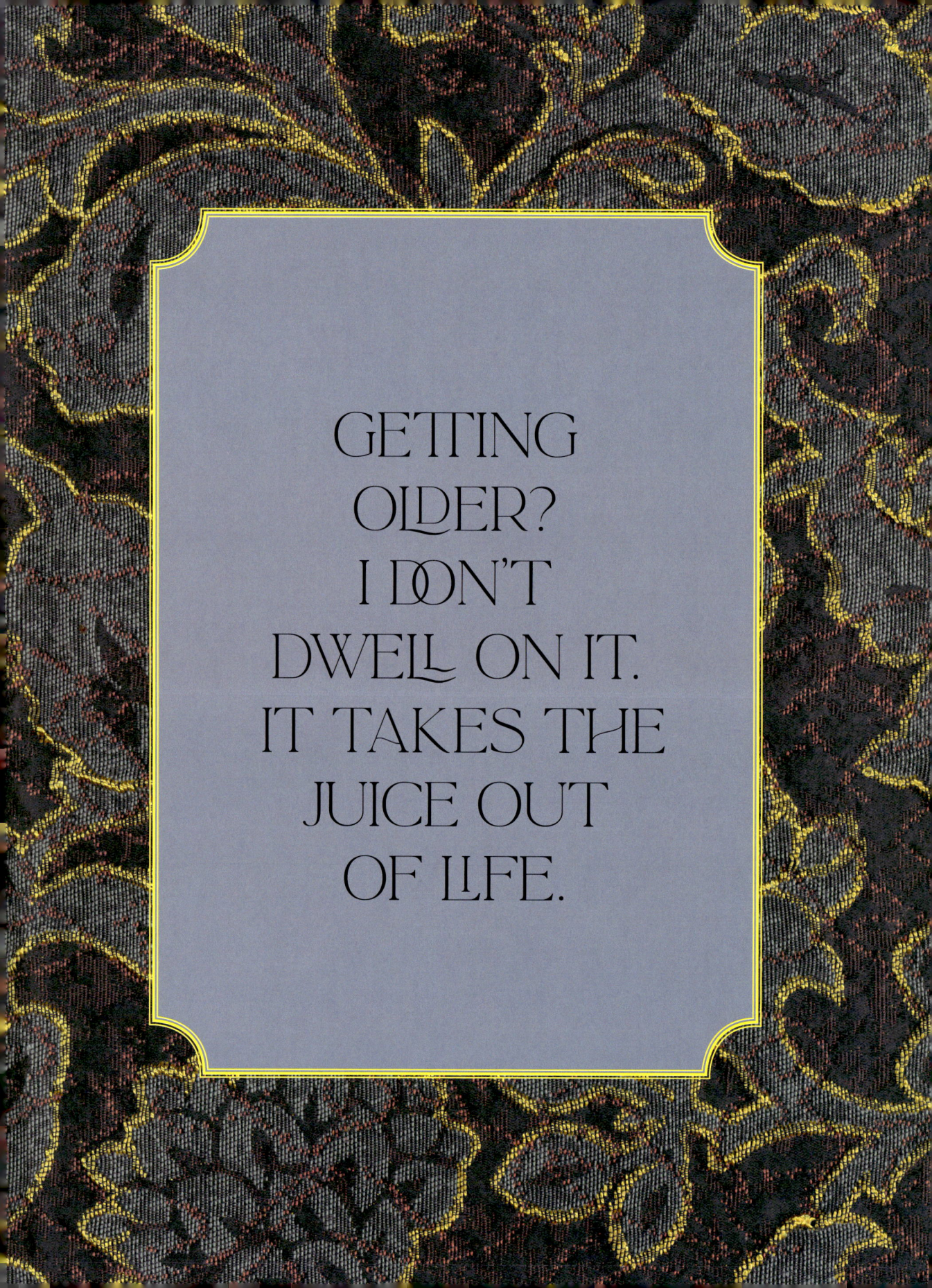

I'm proud of the fact that I've lasted this long – but, really, when I think about my age, it's a passing thought.

I'm all for the future. Maybe that's the thing. I don't fret too much. It's a number. Just because a number comes up doesn't mean you have to stop. It's a matter of the way you look at things. I know 30-year-olds who seem old and 90-year-olds who are young. I just do what I want to do, hoping I can keep getting up in the morning and moving around. As I like to say, *'I'm vertical!'* – that's always a piece of good luck. Good health is the most important thing, because without it you can't do anything.

Getting old ain't for sissies, it's true. But age happens. I feel I'm lucky to be here to capture it. You should give thanks for every year you get. You might start falling apart, but you have to keep going, keep pasting yourself together. To paraphrase an old family friend, *'If you have two of anything, chances are one of them is going to hurt when you get up in the morning.'* I've had two hip operations.

Don't get me wrong, I enjoy my bed. But you must get up. Ageing is a fact of life and when your mind is busy, you don't hurt so much.

You can't stop living and roll up into a ball.

FOR ZENNI OPTICAL
RUVÉN AFANADOR
2021

I have to take a beat every once in a while, but I'm a black belt multitasker. It's so important to be busy. I've seen it so many times with my own eyes – people retire and then one day they wake up and realise how empty their lives are. It isn't funny; people tell me all the time I should be resting, but I feel like I have no time to waste.

It's so important to be passionate about what you do, and I feel blessed that I've had all these different opportunities at this stage in my life: designing, modelling, speaking, teaching, travelling. If someone had told me when I was young that I'd end up here, I would have laughed.

Even if chances come your way, you still must push yourself a little.

If I get up and push myself, I get lost in what I'm doing, and I forget about everything else until I stop doing it. Then I go home and it hurts again, but it's a price worth paying. You may not like getting older, but what's the alternative?

You've got to live in the present. You're here. Embrace it. Live it up.

You know, the other big plus is that you need no longer worry about how you look in a bikini (or whatever your preference is). That, to me, is worth at least ten summers.

Take every chance to celebrate.

I've had some memorable parties in my time, but some stand out more than others. One time, we were visiting a factory in Florence for a furniture project, a collection of wooden furniture I was working on. Our host greeted me and asked me how I was. I said, *'Old'*. He asked why. *'Because it's my birthday.'* He leapt into action. He clapped his hands, called everyone to stop their work and said, *'Facciamo una festa!'* Which means *'We'll make a holiday!'* There was a grocery store with a little restaurant in the back overlooking the valley. It was so charming. He called them up and had them lay on a lunch for everyone. It was just wonderful. So impromptu.

Why not celebrate?

I don't think there's any one secret to longevity, but as I've said before: if you want to stay young, you have to think young.

You need to be able to look at all the silly little things and see how foolish they are. It's not easy when you don't always feel peppy, but you have to try. It's like a muscle. Having a sense of wonder, a sense of humour, and a sense of curiosity are absolutely my tonic. They keep you open to new people and things, always ready for another adventure.

My grandparents and parents were world travellers before jet-setting was invented, so I'm sure it's in my blood. When I think of my grandparents and those epic journeys on those steamers and then, once they reached America, going to and fro across the Hudson for the necessities of life … they didn't look back and neither did I. Looking to the horizon was always going to be part of me.

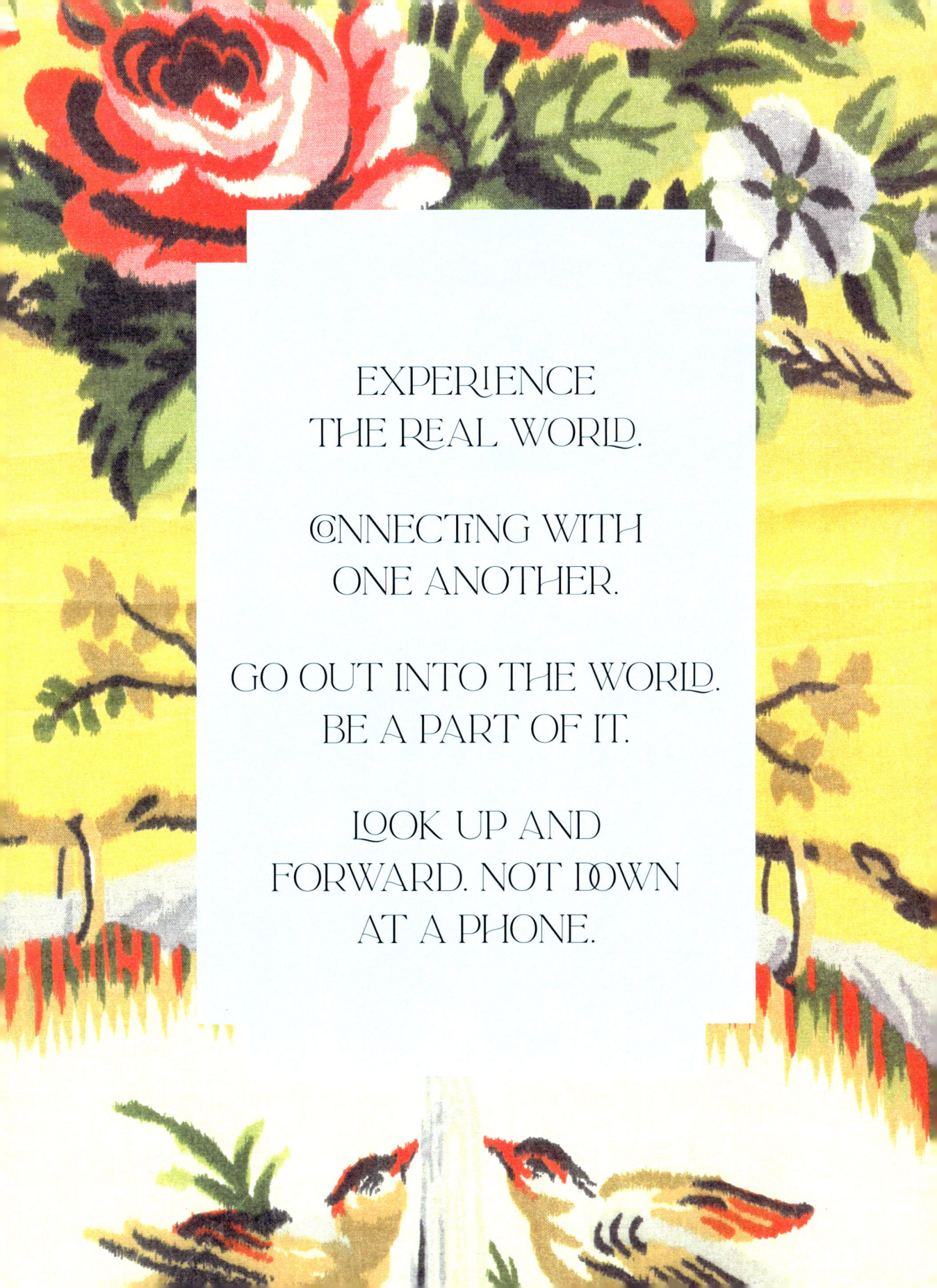

The worst that can happen when you take a risk is that you fail. Be alive. It's about the journey in the end.

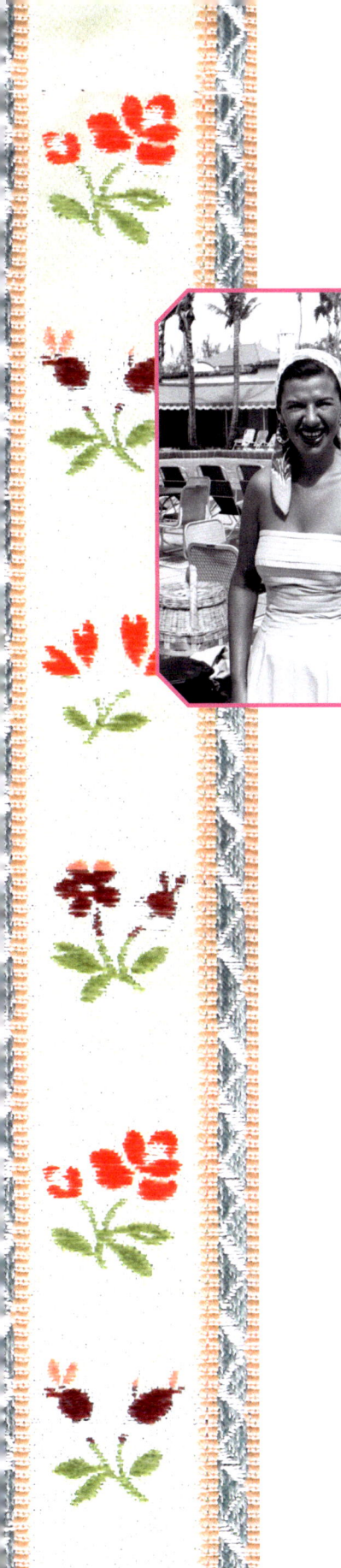

From the earliest trips to Europe with my parents, and then when I started going with Carl ♡, we always went by sea until the liners stopped sailing. Flying, even when it was an option, just wasn't the same. Sailing on the Italian liners – oh, that feeling of crossing the gangplank! It made me so happy. What a rush. We realised that if we went on the American ships, we felt like we were at home until we stepped off the boat at our destination – some people would love that, but we wanted to roam right away. If you took the Italian Line, you were in Italy from the off.

We had so many magical moments on the water. Drifting into port towns the world over, feeling the buzz of life and the promise of adventure coming closer. Even the promise of boats that you can't see would set something stirring inside me. The tiny alleys in Venice that are always a bit wet …

Even now I love the vibrant cities of New York, London and Paris, but also the feeling of peace and escape that I get in Tuscany, Umbria or Palm Beach. But it didn't really matter where it was, it was about going places. Enjoying the ride.

When I was a kid, I was a railroad buff. I still am. I guess I was always destined for a life on the rails.

Going places. A big journey of discovery. Wherever I went, getting there was half the fun.

I'm still a little obsessed with transportation. There's a little Christmas railway set that goes round my Palm Beach apartment all year round. I have a pair of black denim jeans that I bought because they remind me of a railroad man. These things find me.

There's this artist, this kid, whose work we used to buy when we went to Santa Fe every summer. He was about 14 when we first met him. He's Navajo and his sister used to help him dress these little figures. Every year I'd buy a couple. Years later I took them all out and realised that this guy was as hung up on transportation as I am. Every one of the little figures is going someplace. Maybe that's why I kept going back.

It's crazy when I think about how many of the important moments in my life have involved a train ride. At 12, spending five cents on that subway ride from Astoria to S. Klein in Manhattan on the quest for my Easter finery. As I got older and bolder, taking a fancy to New York City and – because in those days you could ride the whole subway system on a nickel – taking a different section of the city each week to explore. Every Thursday I left school early and roamed about Harlem, Yorkville, Chinatown, Greenwich Village. Falling in love with the Village and buying my first piece of costume jewellery. Sneaking off to Chicago to see Duke and his band. Stepping off the train in Palm Beach with seven pieces of old luggage and one new husband.

Sometimes I took a wrong turn, but even then I was lucky. When I found Loehmann's I was following an interior client's directions and got off at the wrong subway stop, in a rainstorm. I was lost, but then, walking into that cavernous wonderland, I was found! I'll never forget catching sight of the store window with a Tiffany glass screen and an outfit by Norman Norell. I had arrived.

I guess what I'm saying is take the trip. I've had a very interesting life because I was willing to take chances. You never know what you'll discover at each stop along the way. You never know where it will lead you.

That time I followed Duke and his band to Chicago, I was supposed to get the train back to Wisconsin, but decided that I'd do some shopping while I was there. I was in possession of four weeks' allowance – my mother was often in arrears with it, occupied with other matters, but luckily this time I was flush. Off I went to Marshall Field's to buy myself a pair of large hoop earrings and a turban. I got waylaid at the book shop on my way to the millinery department. There were these huge tables laden with volumes of English and American poetry. Curiosity won. Two hours later all my loot was gone but I boarded the train with 12 books. I reasoned it was better to put something in my head than on my head.

I think there's a lesson in that. It's incumbent upon you to put something into your head.

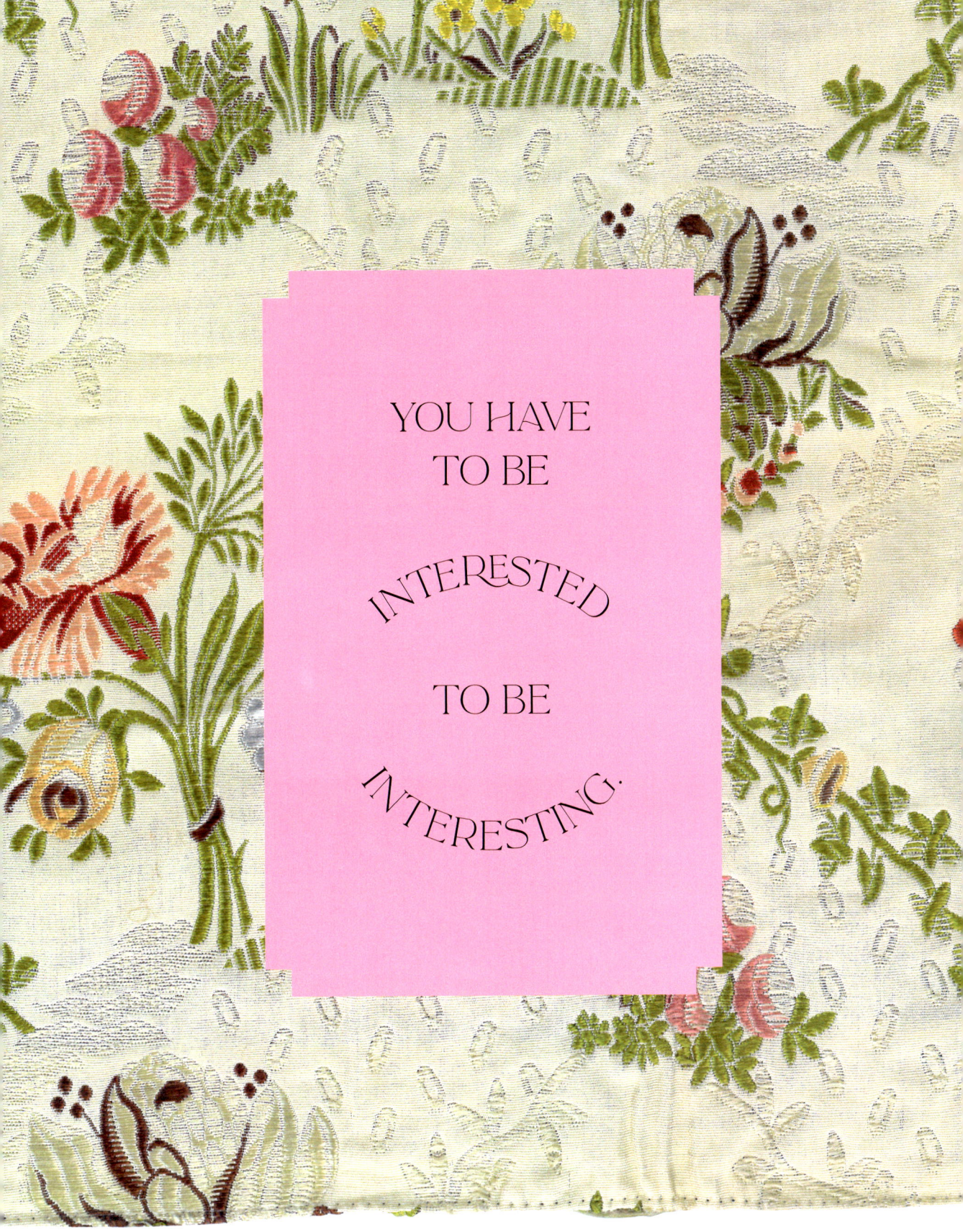

YOU ONLY HAVE ONE TRIP. ENJOY IT

Even now, I love fashion very much, but it's just one part of my life. Many things are more important than fashion. Education. Charity. Doing a good job at whatever your own craft is. Honing that craft. Learning is very important, always. And when you stop learning, that's it.

That's why people get old. They just stop learning. They think they know everything.

Some young people think they were born knowing everything too. That's always the way.

Use your imagination. All the colour is in the world around you. Don't miss it. Open your eyes and your mind to it.

Don't want everything right away. It's a bit like the online shopping thing – buying clothes without trying them on, touching the fabric. Don't get lazy.

My 'overnight' fame took seven decades. Sometimes it's just the right time for things. Don't wait for others to tell you what to do – that makes everyone all alike. You've got to go out and find out for yourself. Get to know yourself. Try to become an individual so you can make your own decisions. You've got to work hard. Research is important for everything. That's why it made me so happy, when my Met Institute exhibit was on, to see fashion students sketching, lying on the floor every morning – you couldn't walk through the room. Those kids had the right idea. When you look harder, you get an extra dimension. You learn about life.

I used to read madly. I never read only one book at a time. I always read at least three at a time. I don't like just one kind of thing. And I'm a multitasker. I found it much more interesting to have a couple of things going at one time. Some books I read to feel calm. Some books I read for excitement. But almost every book, I tried to learn something. I love to look at the books. I take them out and pet them and look at the pictures, and then I put them back, because they're so full of treasures. From every book you learn something. It's never too late.

My father knew everything about some things and something about everything. He was an intellectual, but street-smart, which is a very rare combination. He constantly read Shakespeare and the philosophers, but he was a mass of contradictions, so he loved a good gamble as well. He told me once not to go through life expecting anything from anybody, so that I wouldn't be disappointed, which is very good advice. I had to make my own way.

Mama went to law school and was very unusual for her time, as I said before. She was brilliant in business and refused to use a calculator, even in her final years, lest it dim her wits. When I was young, we lived in a kind of compound where my grandma ruled the roost and Mama never kept house. She didn't sew, or cook, or bake like my aunties, but she knew how to make money. She worked long hours, which left little time for me.

Although I found it hard at the time, I understand that it turned me into the self-reliant person that I am – and a world-class shopper too. I understood that if I wanted clothes I'd have to ferret them out on my own. I was a pragmatist. My mother talked to her stockbrokers every day until she died three weeks shy of her hundredth birthday. She stayed on top of things, stayed curious.

I still have so much to do and a lot more to give. I say put your experience to work, give something back to other people. I've found that work is very healthy for me.

I never want to retire. I enjoy work. I think hard work is my medicine, my salvation.

I meet interesting, creative people (keeping the company of young people helps), my creative juices flow and I really have a fine time. It was very important for me to have work, especially when I lost my husband. If I didn't have work, I think I would go bonkers. Work is exhilarating.

I put my heart and soul into it and it feeds me. I push myself until I can't anymore, and then I come back again for more. I don't use the computer, though, and I don't do email. Technologically, I live in the late-seventeenth century, which I find very comforting. I don't find modern technology friendly. I prefer a candle and a quill instead.

When people ask for my email address I say, 'Darling, send a pigeon.' People go through all kinds of shenanigans to find me, sometimes – but the ones who do get through, I know they're serious. It can make them a bit grumpy, but c'est la vie.

Focus on cultivating your inner life.

I'm a private person. Privacy is very precious. Someone who can tell a great story, or someone with great humour – a spark – is memorable, and I don't care if anyone else knows who they are. I don't look for recognition. If you start seeking validation outside of yourself, that's not a good place to be.

People come to me because they're interested in doing something creative, fun things, working with me, and that's great, but I don't look for it. Attention takes a bit of getting used to, but I've tried to direct it into positive things. It's very flattering that people post pictures and drawings they've done of me – I even know of one girl who had a tattoo of me on her wrist. It's a very good portrait! I hope that's because I inspire them in a meaningful way. We were all put here on this planet to do something. Forget celebrity, but if you're a positive role model for someone, that's great.

I've had the opportunity to collaborate with so many wonderful creative people. But more importantly I can help people, which is very rewarding, whether it's through a charitable cause or by making lovely, uplifting, joyful things. Helping people put themselves together is very important to me. Teaching young fashion students and seeing them grow has been wonderful.

I love giving back. If life is good to you, you have to give back.

If you can help someone have a better life, that's just wonderful. Because you only have one trip.

If you're happy, have found love, are surrounded by good people, doing what you like and giving back to others, that's success.

You also have to know when you've got a good thing. My philosophy is, there's no free lunch. The day I realised that I felt I'd grown up. Everything has a price. It isn't always money, it could be time or experience, or it could be love. But you don't get anything for nothing.

I never had a plan. If it happens, it happens. You have to be open.

You will miss a lot of things, but you can't do everything.

You can't have it all. You're setting yourself up for regrets if you think that you can. It's not possible. I learned that a long time ago.

Sometimes you have to choose. People become nervous wrecks because they think they can and should do everything. It's such a shame.

—⁓—

My mother was a graduate of the New York University and was in law school when she got pregnant with me. She had to stop studying. In those days, that's how it was. She gave up ten years of her life to raise me. When she went back to work I was so upset. I thought she had forsaken me. I was so young and I didn't understand that it was the Depression, and it had to be done. At the time it felt terrible.

Much later I realised that she had been decades ahead of her time.

Most women then didn't work. My mother was brave. She made choices and she owned them.

→ ME STEPPING INTO LIFE, WORK, THE FUTURE.
It was all waiting.

She was a crackerjack businesswoman. I came to the realisation – long overdue – that it was my darling mother that was my model all these years, despite our superficial differences. She eventually became my closest, dearest friend.

I wanted a career, I wanted to travel, and I wanted to work hard. I didn't want to have a child and then have that child raised by a nanny, which would have been the option for me at that time with all the travelling. I never like to be pigeonholed and I didn't like the fact that I'd have to do things in a certain way. I didn't want to be held back from living life my way. I couldn't have it all. Something must give and sometimes it's you. Life is full of choices. No one said they were all going to be easy ones.

But you're lucky

if you get to choose.

YOU ONLY HAVE ONE TRIP. ENJOY IT

6
THERE'S ALL KINDS OF BEAUTY

On appreciation

I am constantly on a quest for beautiful things. I'll never stop searching or collecting. But that pursuit of beauty has never been about personal beauty. At least not since I was four years old, yearning for blonde curls I would never have.

When Mrs Loehmann told me all those years ago that I was no beauty, but that having style was better, I don't think I fully understood her meaning. But as the years passed I realised how right she was.

In my experience, working on your sense of style lifts you up, but the heavy ideals of beauty, of prettiness, can bring you down.

FOR *Harper's Bazaar Arabia*
RICHARD PHIBBS
2021

Don't misunderstand me – prettiness is nice if you have it. I'm not saying don't make an effort. Putting in a little effort is good, spending a little time on yourself. There are certain things I know look more attractive on me than others, and my hair looks better done in certain ways. It's a lot of fun to be glamorous. I like a lot of pigment in my lipstick! We've all done a little smoke and mirror work. And as I said before, nothing exists in a vacuum, so of course style and beauty are connected.

I think a good use of energy is keeping it fun. I always used very simple things on my skin. Any time I did something like get a facial I'd come home laden with expensive product and then never use it. I haven't got time.

When I was younger, I wore the same very bright mouth that I do now, but with heavy eye makeup too. Designing my own makeup collection later in life, with Ciaté London, was like a mad, psychedelic dream. The fun I had playing with the colours …

I used that trick for a long time with eyeshadow and bright lipstick.

I'm not very good at putting on makeup, but lips are easy. That flash of colour suits my personality.

One summer when I was about 18, my friend's older sister, who was a very glamorous fashion model, took me in hand. She had a tube of black moustache wax. She struck a match and melted some of the wax in a spoon, then quickly applied it to my

eyelashes. It looked like very heavy mascara, and I had long lashes so the effect was very striking. A bit like Miss Piggy. At the time, we thought it sinfully wicked and très, très sexy.

Without the element of self-expression, prettiness for its own sake is unimportant.

Be memorable for other reasons! The young ladies I went to school with who had the perfect hair, the prom queens, it took up so much of their time and attention. As they got older, when some of the prettiness faded, they didn't have anything to fall back on, and they got more and more disappointed, more upset. They forgot to grow in other ways.

When you're like me, attractiveness is something you cultivate. You have to develop something else to get where you want to go. You have to learn and do things. So you become a bit more interesting. When you get older, that goes a long way.

Beauty is not only in the eye of the beholder, it is largely in your head.

So many people try, consciously or unconsciously, to emulate others. Attractiveness doesn't work that way. What a waste of energy. Spend time learning how to express your individual self. It's the same with writing, cooking or anything else. It's common sense – it's not magic. It just takes a bit of effort.

Every culture does it differently, and the standards of beauty – what's considered beautiful – change over time. It doesn't just mean one thing. If you think about it, there's raw beauty, artificial beauty, sweet beauty, old-fashioned beauty and sexy beauty. Sometimes we look back at the past and we can't understand the beauty ideals of the time. It's all about a point of view.

It comes back to confidence in the end. If you look uncomfortable in your own skin, it shows.

There's a lot to be said for serenity. It's one of the most beautiful looks there is.

THERE'S ALL KINDS OF BEAUTY

Everything is your attitude. When you think about things a certain way, you look a certain way. And I think that's why I've never got the plastic surgery thing. It's a fantastic invention if, God forbid, you're in an accident or have some kind of trauma, but using it to get nipped and tucked and look younger … I don't understand it.

Sometimes when Carl ♡ and I went out, he used to look around and say,

'Baby, you're the only one here with your own face.'

To me, wrinkles are a badge of courage. There's nothing wrong with them.

My biggest achievement is lasting this long! Why try to hide the years you've been lucky enough to live? If you get more years, that's wonderful. Celebrate it.

Nobody is going to think you're 30 if you get a facelift at 70. You're not fooling anyone. To subject yourself to something painful and very expensive when you never know how it's going to turn out is a risk – you could end up worse than you started.

People used to say to me that I should go blonde. I used to get so much abuse for my hair! Fortunately, Carl ♡ liked grey hair, so I wasn't tempted to colour it. I've been grey since almost forever. I had black hair with a wide white streak in it, a bit like a skunk. My mother always did her hair and I guess her daughter having grey hair made her feel older, but I refused to dye it. I bought a coat and a Russian steppes-style hat from Lanvin in the same streaky grey as my hair – it was wild and it stopped New York traffic. You couldn't tell where the outfit ended and I began. My hair then turned from pepper and salt to grey, and then, finally, it turned white.

← MY MOTHER AND ME, DRESSING FOR DINNER SOMEWHERE FUN.

I have to give great thanks to the man upstairs. If you live long enough, doctors treat you like a coddled egg, but I just try to be as careful as possible. I have kept healthy. There's no big secret to it. I don't live a crazy life, but when you're travelling all around the place you do have to keep some sort of routine, so I got used to that. I eat the same breakfast every day, wherever I am in the world.

I'm not much of a cook, I admit, but I always ate wholesome food. I think I told you I'm very partial to one particular pizza, but I trained myself not to eat junk food. I don't believe in trends of any kind. The healthiest diet is just to push yourself away from the table. I don't drink soda. I have alcohol now and then. I used to be a heavy smoker – four packs a day! I just quit one day. I'd exercise periodically. I think working hard kept me active. And these days I enjoy being at home too. I'm very self-sufficient, which helped during the pandemic. I was in Italy during their cholera epidemic many decades ago, so it wasn't my first time, but that was nothing like this one.

⌒ᴧᴧ⌒

I have an apartment on a lake and a lovely terrace that sits out on the water. I love to lie there on the chaise and stare out into space. I'm so grateful that I have it; it's beautiful. I do a lot of writing and it's very pleasant to work wearing one of my many, many robes, and not getting dressed.

If I never had a reason to get dressed up, I'd feel very bad. But all those years, I never really dressed up when I was at home because I was at home so rarely. It feels like a luxury to dress up at home. Although I won't say no to a nice, cuddly, white terrycloth robe.

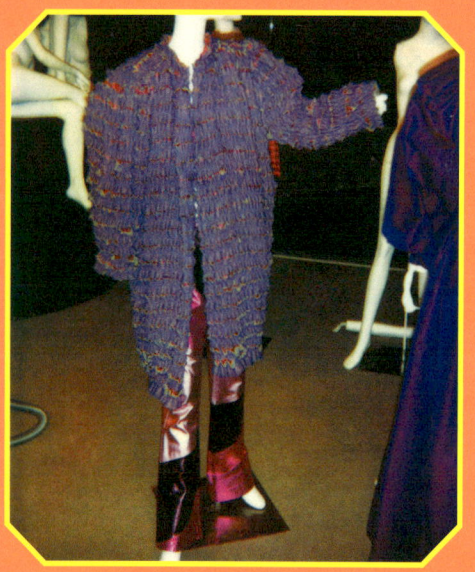

My so-called collection is my wardrobe. It has everything from the simple and zen or serious, to madly baroque or amusing. I always buy things to wear, not to collect them. I've been the same size since high school, so it's a big collection. After the Costume Institute show at The Met, the exhibition toured several places. The show at Peabody Essex Museum in Salem Massachusetts was one of the proudest moments of my life.

It was one of the curators there who first likened my approach to dressing and accessorising to the improvisation of jazz.

It made so much sense to me. The Peabody has a very special place in my heart. They have their own excellent costume collection, but we realised that the timeline of theirs stopped exactly around the time that mine began. Every year since, they have visited me and we determine which pieces they are going to take away. It's not easy deciding what to give away.

←   **MY COLLECTION ON SHOW**

Here are a few of my favourite outfits that appeared in the Costume Institute show at The Met and later at the Peabody Essex Museum in Salem, Massachusetts.

FROM FRIEND AND CREATOR

Fern Mallis

'Iris is the whole rainbow.
The supersize Crayola box.
She's a Pantone® swatch book.
One day she's a vision in turquoise,
covered in layers of jewellery, the next
day it's shocking pink from head
to toe ... then sunny yellow.
She wears colour

like no one else.'

My clothes are the

People ask me what my favourite pieces are and, to me, it feels a bit like asking someone, *who's your favourite child?* They all mean something. It's not easy to part with something that has a memory attached to it, and in some cases I'm sorry to see them go.

But, as you get older, you realise that all these 'things' are just things, and to give them away could brighten someone's life. To be part of the stories of their life is a wonderful notion.

stories of my life.

IRIS FOR ZENNI OPTICAL
RUVÉN AFANADOR
2021

OLD WORLD WEAVERS
Silk Fabrics for the Connoisseur
979 Third Ave., New York, N.Y 10022, 355-7186-7
Chicago • Dallas • Atlanta • Los Angeles
San Francisco • Seattle • Houston • Denver
Miami • Palm Beach • Washington, D.C.
Toronto • Boston

LONGUEVILLE

NO. F-13380

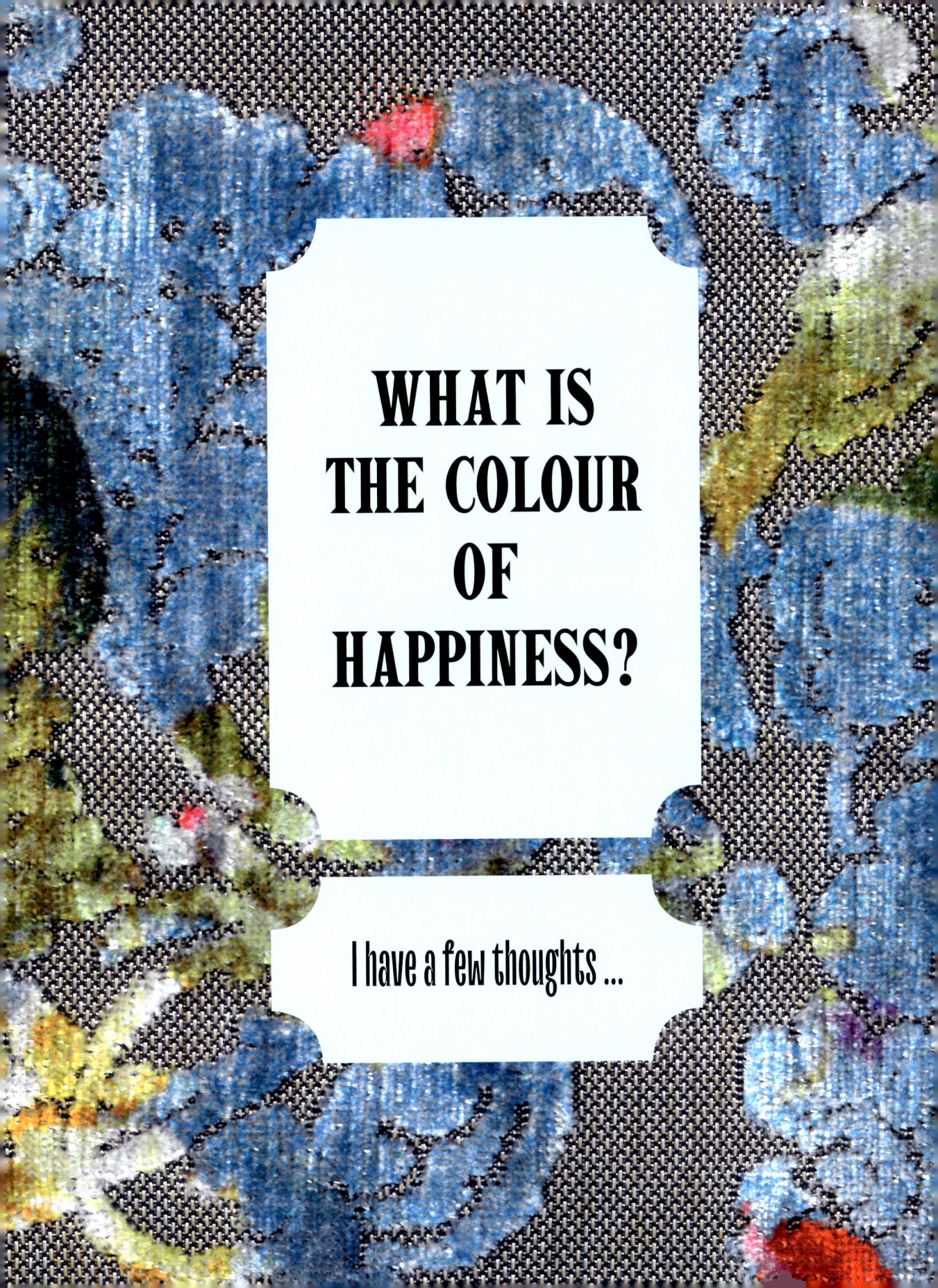

PUT ON 👓 YOUR GLASSES

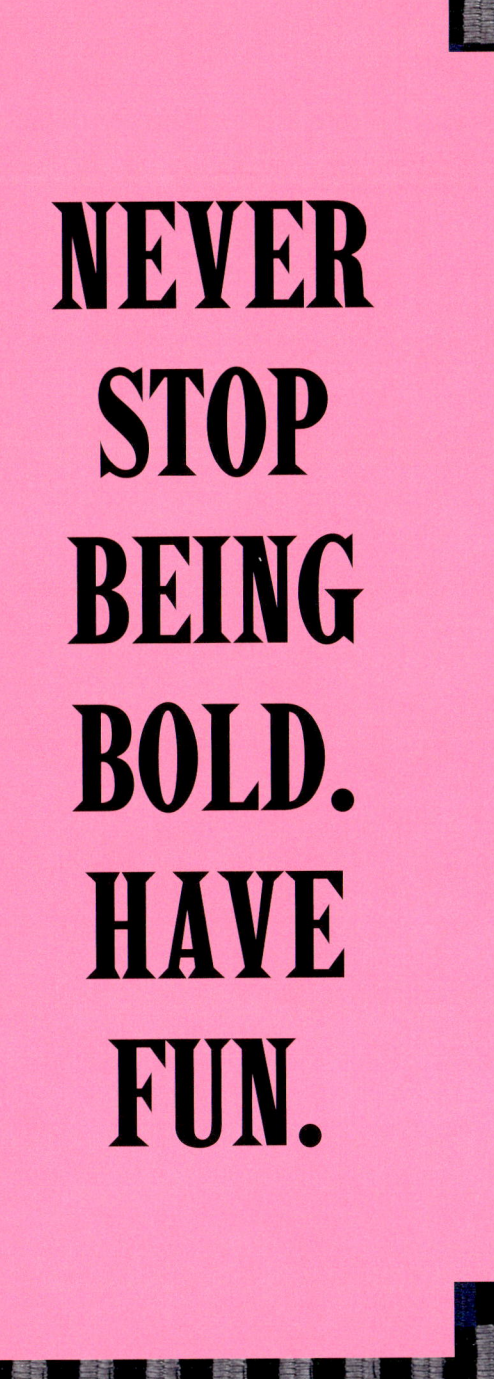

GET COMFORTABLE OUTSIDE YOUR COMFORT ZONE.

Enjoy the trip.

THE
SEARCH
FOR
WISDOM
CONTINUES...

Index

Page numbers in *italics* refer to illustrations

A

accessories 61, 116, 119
ACE Awards, New York *110*
Afanador, Ruvén *18*, *128*, 129
Africa, North *20*, 23, 123, 124–5
ageing 212–43, 275
Amsterdam 122
animals 47, 155
   animal prints 36, *43*
Apfel, Carl (Pussycat) 134
   colours *88–9*, 89, 97
   death 144, 217, 236
   glasses 77
   Iris's clothes 41, 204
   Iris's collection 68
   Iris's reaction to fabrics 119
   marriage to Iris 96, 108, 137–48, 151, 200, 217, 229, 255, 256
   New Mexico 59
   Old World Weavers 32
   travels *20–1*, 23, 28, 108, *112*, 113, 119–27, 120, 146, 204–5, 227
   watches 163
Apfel, Iris
   bargain hunting 63–70
   collection 40, 68, 260–3
   colours 80–129, 134
   and Duke Ellington 173–4
   glasses *10*, *18*, *69*, 70–7, 268
   grandparents 63, 64, 141, *194*, 195–202, 224, 235
   hair 256
   hats 113, *113*, 115
   healthy lifestyle 257
   influence of father on 34–6, 64
   influence of Millicent Rogers on 59
   influence of Mrs Loehmann on 55–7
   influence of mother on 61–4, 242
   interest in fabric 203–5
   interior design 64, 166–8, 177
   jeans 112, 206–7, 228
   jewellery 59, 67, *162–3*, 163
   loves of 64, 155
   makeup 247, 248–50
   marriage to Carl 96, 108, 137–48, 151, 200, 217, 229, 255, 256
   nature as influence 42–52
   Old World Weavers 28, 32, 40, *57*, 203
   origin of style 114
   reading 233
   train journeys 227–30
   travels *20–1*, 23, 24, 27, 28, *35*, 108, *112*, 113, 119–27, 146, 204–5, 227–30, 257
   University of Wisconsin 171–4
   wedding dress 96
   work 236
   Zenni Optical *18*, 25, 76–7, 85, *109*, 187, 220, 265
appreciation 247–65
art 34
Art Nouveau 36
Asofsky family (Iris's grandparents) 63, 64, 141, *194*, 195–202, 224, 235
Astoria 200–1, 229
attractiveness 250–2
Avedon, Richard 129

B

Barcelona 122
bargain hunting 63–70
Barhep Imports and Exports Corp 64
baroque 36
Barrel, Sadye (Iris's mother) 36, *36*, 47, 60
   ballet 34
   colours 84, *86–7*, 87
   education and work 235, 240–2
   hair 256
   influence on Iris 61–4, 242
   Iris's clothes 204
   Iris's trip to Chicago 174
   little black dresses 99
   travel *35*
   zebra skin 50
Barrel, Samuel (Iris's father) 36, 63, *86–7*
   colours *86–7*, 87
   confidence 189
   influence on Iris 34–6, 64
   knowledge 234
   travel *35*, 64
   work 64
beauty 244–65, 274
Beirut 124
Berlin 122
birds 47, 155
Bittar, Alexis 211
black 99
blue
   denim blue 112
   teal blue 112
   turquoise 101, 108–10
boldness 133–83, 271
Bonwit Teller 137, 138
boots 155
Bowery 168
Brooklyn 201
Bursa 120
butterflies *52*
Byzantine Empire 37

C

Capri 113, *113*, 123
Caserta 123
celebrations 224
Chambi, Martin 129
Chicago 173–4, 229, 230
child, inner 135, 154
choice 242–3
clothing
   investment pieces 96
   little black dress 99
   colours 80–129, 134
   black 99
   colour pops 99, 248

combining bright colours 101–5
denim blue 112
emerald green 101, 110
green 101, 110, 113, 182
importance of 12–13
layering 48
lime green 101
orange 101
pink 96, 106, 113
pops of 116
red 101, 106–8
teal blue 112
tonality 93
turquoise 101, 108–10
violet 101, 112
yellow 38, 101, 211
comfort zones 184–211, 272
confidence 186–211
Costume Institute, Metropolitan Museum of Art 147, 233, 260
courage 186–211
creativity 19, 168–9
influence and 16–79
Crete 126
cultural influences 34
curiosity 224, 235
Czardas Rug *51*

D
D'Aras, Mr 66–7
denim blue 112
design, and style 30–1
Dr. Scholl's Shoes *158–9*
Doria Pamphilj Palace 123
dresses, little black 99
dressing up 119, 150
Dublin 147

E
Ellington, Duke 173–4, 215, 229, 230
emerald green 101, 110
emotions, colour and 106
Englander, Arthur 137–8
Europe 20–1, 23, 28, 67, 119, 227
expense, style and 67
experiences 14, 19
expression, freedom of 179
eyewear *10*, *69*, 70–7, 268
Zenni Optical *18*, *25*, 76–7, *85*, *109*, *187*, *220*, *265*

F
failure 226
fashion, as a mirror of society 153
fear of judgement 186
feathers *42*, 155
flea markets 41, 70, 147
Florence 224
flowers 47
Flutterby Rug *52*
France *57*, 119
freedom of expression 179
fun 131–69, 186, 248, 271
furniture 224
furs 155

G
Gaudí, Antoni 122
gemstone colours 93
giving back 239
glasses *10*, *69*, 70–7, 268
Zenni Optical *18*, *25*, 76–7, *85*, *109*, *187*, *220*, *265*
Goodman, Benny 172
Grand Bazaar, Istanbul 120
Grand Hotel Quisisana 113
green 113, 182
emerald green 101, 110
lime green 101
Greenwich Village 66–7, 229
Gussie 161
gut instinct 179, 180

H
H&M 38, 110
happiness, colour of 266–77
Harper's Bazaar 80, *183*
Harper's Bazaar Arabia 10, *192*, *246*
Harry Winston 163
hats 113, *113*, 115
Hilfiger, Tommy 80, 81
Hong Kong 122
houses 166–8, 177
humour 61, 101, 134, 147, 154, 204–6, 224
Hungarian patterns *51*

I
imagination 232
improvisation 168, 170–4, 176
India 28–9
influence 16–79
nature as 42–52
inner child 135, 154
inspiration 16–79, 238–9, 269

nature as 42–52
interests 231–7, 250
interior design 166–8, 177
inventiveness 67
investment pieces 96
Ireland 122, 147
Istanbul 120
Italy 123, 204–6, 227, 257–8

J
jazz 39, 116, 155, 172–4, 176, 260
Duke Ellington 173–4, 215, 229, 230
jeans 112, 206–7, 228
jewellery
Native American 59
playful jewellery *162–3*, 163
statement jewellery 59
Johnson, Elinor 168
journeys 226
joy 153
judgement, fear of 186

K
Kahlo, Frida 123
Kermit 161
Koda, Harold 147
Konrath, Andreas Laszlo *132*

L
Lanvin 106, 256
laughter 133, 134, 154
learning 230–7, 250
Liebman, Jeremy *100*
lime green 101
living in the now 148, 215, 222

INDEX

279

Loehmann, Mrs *54, 55–7, 247*
Loehmann's *54, 55–7, 56, 229*
L'Officiel Paris 100
London 28, 70, 122, 227
Long Island City 200–1
longevity 212–43, 275

M
makeup 247, 248–50
Mame, Auntie 19
Marché aux Puces 41
Marshall Field's 230
Matisse, Henri 39
Maysles, Albert 144
Metropolitan Museum of Art 147, 233, 260
Mexico City 122–3
Mickey Mouse 160–1
Middle East 124
Milan 123
Millicent Rogers Museum 59
Morocco 126

N
Nance, Ray 173
Naples 123, 124
Native American jewellery 59
nature 42–52
Neiman Marcus 137
New York City 227, 229
New York Dress Institute 58
New York University 171
  School of Advertising 144
Norell, Norman 153, 229

North Africa 20, 23, 123, 124–5

O
oceans 47, 112
Old World Weavers 203
  inspiration for 32, 41
  Lyonnaise velvet priest's tunic fabric 41
  research trips 28, *57*
  textile designs 40–1
Olowu, Duro 24
orange 101
originality 190–1

P
Palm Beach 155, 161, 227, 228, 229
Paris 119, 227
parties 224
passion 221
past, living in the 148, 215, 222
pastels 84
pattern 14, 19, 23–4
  animal prints 36, *43*
  layering 48
  what makes a good pattern 31
Peabody Essex Museum 260
Penn, Irving 129
personality 23, 153
  colour and 12
Phibbs, Richard 10, *42, 80, 183*
pink 96, 106, 113
plants 47
plastic surgery 255–6

playfulness 133–83
Plaza Hotel 138
present, living in the 148, 215, 222
prettiness 247, 250
priest's tunic, Lyonnaise velvet 41
privacy 238
procrastination 19

R
Ray, Man 106
reading 233
red 101, 106–8
research 233
risk 179, 226
Rivera, Diego 123
Rogers, Millicent *58, 59, 59,* 108
role models 238–9
Rucci, Ralph 24
Ruggable 50
rugs
  Czardas Rug *51*
  Flutterby Rug *52*
  zebra print *50*

S
Santa Fe 228
self-expression 189
serenity 253
Sheppard, Eugenia 41
shoes, Dr. Scholl's Shoes *156–9*
shopping on a shoestring 64
Sidi Bou Said 125
Siena 126

Sinatra, Frank 215
smiling 154
society, fashion as a mirror of 153
Steinberg, Saul 155
Strayhorn, Billy 215
Sturman, Christopher *117, 118, 167*
style 56, 114
  and beauty 247–8
  courage and 190
  and design 30–1
  and expense 67
  and knowing who you are 61
  as manifestation of your spirit 23
Summerton, Emma *214*

T
Tangier 125
Tate Modern 39
teal blue 112
texture 14, 19
tonality 93
Toulouse-Lautrec, Henri 56
travel, as inspiration 27–9
trends 153
Tunisia 124
Turkish towels 120
turquoise 101, 108–10
Tuscany 227

U
Umbria 227
University of Wisconsin 171–3

V

validation, seeking 238

Venice 123, 227

Versace, Gianni 24

violet 101, 112

Vreeland, Diana 166

W

Waldorf Astoria 138, *138*, 141

Weber, Bruce 182

white and black combinations 99

the White House 40, *40*, 41

Whiteside, Thomas *104*

work 61, 235–6, 273

wrinkles 255

Y

yellow 38, 101, 211

young people 236

Z

zebra print 50

Zenni Optical *18, 25, 76–7, 85, 109, 187, 220, 265*

Picture credits

With special thanks to Ruvén Afanador and Richard Phibbs, and creative partners Ruggable, Zenni, Ciaté London and Dr. Scholl's Shoes for kindly sharing a number of photographs included in this book.

All photography, not listed below, comes from Iris's personal archive © Iris Apfel.

Textile designs are from the Old World Weavers archive © Iris Apfel with the exception of pages 50, 51 and 52 © Ruggable.

PRELIMS

1 Iris's 100th birthday portrait, August 2021, by Ruvén Afanador © Iris Apfel

3–4 Iris Apfel x Ruggable launch, November 2022, courtesy of Ruggable © Ruvén Afanador

CHAPTER 1

10 For *Harper's Bazaar Arabia*, September 2021 © Richard Phibbs/Trunk Archive

18 Iris Apfel x Zenni Optical launch, June 2021, courtesy of Zenni Optical, Inc © Ruvén Afanador

22 Iris Apfel attends the American Apparel & Footwear Association's 38th Annual American Image Awards in New York City, May 2016. Photo by Ilya S. Savenok/Getty Images for American Apparel & Footwear Association (AAFA)

25 Having fun with Ruvén, Palm Beach, June 2021 © Ruvén Afanador

38 For *Harper's Bazaar*, August 2021 © Ruvén Afanador

42 For *Harper's Bazaar Arabia*, September 2021 © Richard Phibbs/Trunk Archive

50–52 Iris Apfel x Ruggable launch 2022/2023 © Ruggable

54 Mrs Loehmann courtesy of the Frieda Mueller Trust

58 Millicent Rogers is among the ten best-dressed women of 1947, chosen by the New York Dress Institute in a poll of fashion designer and editors © Bettman/Getty

75–77 From the Iris Apfel x Zenni Optical collection © Zenni Optical, Inc

80 For *Harper's Bazaar Arabia*, September 2021 © Richard Phibbs/Trunk Archive

CHAPTER 2

85 Iris Apfel x Zenni Optical launch, June 2021, courtesy of Zenni Optical, Inc © Ruvén Afanador

92 For *Harper's Bazaar Arabia*, September 2021 © Richard Phibbs/Trunk Archive

94–95 For *Evening Standard*, United Kingdom, November 2012 © Thomas Whiteside/Trunk Archive

100 For *L'Officiel France*, October 2016 © Jeremy Liebman/Trunk Archive

104 For *Evening Standard*, United Kingdom, November 2012 © Thomas Whiteside/Trunk Archive

109 Iris Apfel x Zenni Optical launch, June 2021, courtesy of Zenni Optical, Inc © Ruvén Afanador

110	Iris Apfel attends the 2021 Ace Awards at Cipriani 42nd Street wearing her H&M collection suit, November 2021, in New York © Jamie McCarthy/Getty Images	167	For *Harper's Bazaar Russia*, September 2010 © Christopher Sturman/Trunk Archive
111	For *Harper's Bazaar Arabia*, September 2021 © Richard Phibbs/Trunk Archive	173	American jazz pianist and composer Duke Ellington (1899 - 1974), photographed in 1940 © MPI/Getty Images
117	For *Harper's Bazaar Russia*, September 2010 © Christopher Sturman/Trunk Archive	183	Iris Apfel x Zenni Optical launch, June 2021, courtesy of Zenni Optical, Inc © Ruvén Afanador
118	Iris Apfel x Zenni Optical launch, June 2021, courtesy of Zenni Optical, Inc © Ruvén Afanador		
128	For *FortyFiveTen*, June 2016 © Ruvén Afanador		

CHAPTER 4

187	For *Harper's Bazaar Arabia*, September 2021 © Richard Phibbs/Trunk Archive
192	Iris Apfel x Zenni Optical launch, June 2021, courtesy of Zenni Optical, Inc © Ruvén Afanador
210	For *L'Officiel France*, October 2016 © Jeremy Liebman/Trunk Archive

CHAPTER 3

132	With Carl, for *Süddeutsche Zeitung Magazin*, Germany, February 2011 © Andreas Laszlo Konrath/Trunk Archive
156	Iris Apfel's jewellery for sale at the Peabody Essex Museum, December 2009. Staff photo by Angela Rowlings. (Photo by MediaNews Group/Boston Herald via Getty Images).
157	(TOP)Iris Apfel and Carl Apfel, October 2008, New York City. (Photo by BILLY FARRELL/Patrick McMullan via Getty Images). (BOTTOM) Iris Apfel attends the Couture Council of the museum at FIT's 7th annual award benefit honouring Valentino Garavani, 2011. (Photo by Steve Eichner/WWD/Penske Media via Getty Images)
158–159	Iris Apfel x Dr. Scholl's launch, 2024 © Dr. Scholl's Shoes
164–165	Iris Apfel x Zenni Optical launch, June 2021, courtesy of Zenni Optical, Inc © Ruvén Afanador

CHAPTER 5

214	For Kate Spade, March 2015 © Emma Summerton/Trunk Archive
220	Iris Apfel x Zenni Optical launch, June 2021, courtesy of Zenni Optical, Inc © Ruvén Afanador

CHAPTER 6

246	For *Harper's Bazaar Arabia*, September 2021 © Richard Phibbs/Trunk Archive
248	Iris Apfel x Ciaté London lipstick, September 2022, © Ciaté London
264–265	Iris Apfel x Zenni Optical launch, June 2021, courtesy of Zenni Optical, Inc © Ruvén Afanador

ENDMATTER

286	Iris and Lori, 2023 © Lori Sale

EBURY PRESS, AN IMPRINT
OF EBURY PUBLISHING
20 VAUXHALL BRIDGE ROAD
LONDON SW1V 2SA

Ebury Press is part of the Penguin Random House group of companies whose addresses can be found at global.penguinrandomhouse.com

COPYRIGHT © IRIS APFEL 2024

Iris Apfel has asserted her right to be identified as the author of this Work in accordance with the Copyright, Designs and Patents Act 1988

FIRST PUBLISHED BY EBURY PRESS IN 2024
WWW.PENGUIN.CO.UK

A CIP CATALOGUE RECORD FOR THIS BOOK IS AVAILABLE FROM THE BRITISH LIBRARY

ISBN 9781529916164

DESIGN BY IMAGIST
WWW.IMAGISTLONDON.COM

COLOUR ORIGINATION
BY ALTAIMAGE, LONDON

PRINTED AND BOUND IN CHINA
BY C&C OFFSET PRINTING CO., LTD

Penguin Random House is committed to a sustainable future for our business, our readers and our planet. This book is made from Forest Stewardship Council® certified paper.

FROM FRIEND AND LONG-TIME AGENT

Lori Sale

Iris Apfel is extraordinary. Working alongside her is the honour of a lifetime. Her daily calls, always greeted with the familiar question – 'What have you got for me today?' – are testament to her insatiable desire to work. She is a visionary in every sense of the word. She sees the world through a unique lens – one adorned with giant, distinctive spectacles that sit atop her nose. Through those lenses, she sees the world as a kaleidoscope of colours, a canvas of patterns and prints. Her artistic eye transforms the mundane into the extraordinary and her ability to blend the unconventional with the elegant is nothing short of magical.

Much love,
Iris

Iris Barrel Apfel was born in Astoria, Queens, New York. She was the only child of Samuel Barrel, an artisan who owned a family business, and his wife, Syd, who owned a local fashion boutique.

Iris studied art history at New York University and went on to fine arts school at the University of Wisconsin. After college, Iris joined Women's Wear Daily, in addition to working for noted interior designer, Elinor Johnson.

Iris met her husband, the beloved Carl Apfel (d. 2015), and their first date was on Columbus Day. Mr. Apfel proposed on Thanksgiving, and they were married on President's Day, 22 February 1948.

Iris and Carl collaborated on many business adventures throughout their nearly seventy-year marriage, including working directly with the First Ladies of nine US Presidents in the department of fine art at The White House. In 1950, they started Old World Weavers, an utterly fabulous fabric house, whose designs are still as eye-catchingly ornate today.

Iris travelled the world with Carl – most often for business – exploring new cultures and relishing all the inspiration that it offered. Iris developed a reputation as the whisperer for all things matchless and distinctive, scouring the antique textile booths in Paris, the backstreets of London, the Grand Bazaar of Istanbul, the miraculous souks of the Middle East, and working with Italian artisans.

Collecting a seemingly limitless treasure-trove, she became a legendary lender to exhibitions across the globe, including at The Fashion Institute of Technology, The Peabody-Essex Museum, and The Metropolitan Museum of Art, where the 2005 Rara Avis exhibition of her clothing and accessories launched her to international fame.

Iris is known worldwide as the 'geriatric starlet'. In 2014, she was the subject of director Albert Maysles's award-winning film Iris. In 2018, at the age of ninety-six, she was the oldest person to be turned into a Barbie doll.

Most likely one of the most photographed women in fashion's history, she has worn many hats: textile guru, bespoke interior designer, visiting professor, museum lender, style icon, brand ambassador, and social media celebrity. Iris has been the subject of countless honors, awards, and partnerships with corporations, including with MAC, Mattel, McDonald's, H&M, Hugo Boss, Etsy, Ebay, Ciaté, Ruggable and Zenni. This girl from Astoria certainly has come a long way over the last century.